One Hundred Winters

MAURICE BAMFORD

VERTICAL EDITIONS

www.verticaleditions.com

First published in the United Kingdom in 2009
by Vertical Editions, Unit 4a, Snaygill Industrial Estate,
Skipton, North Yorkshire BD23 2QR

www.verticaleditions.com

ISBN 978-1-904091-33-2

A CIP catalogue record for this book is available
from the British Library

The author would like to thank Graham Morris,
Robert Gate, RLphotos.com and others for their help
with information and the photographs used in this book

Cover design and typeset by HBA, York

Printed and bound by the
Cromwell Press Group, Trowbridge

CONTENTS

INTRODUCTION

This book was not envisaged to be a history of the game, nor does it look at the game through the eyes of a historian. It looks at the game through the eyes of a former player, coach and lifelong enthusiast who is appalled at the apparent disrespect that is shown to the former great traditions and players whose deeds seem to be ignored by modern 'experts'. Rarely are the exploits of these great players mentioned today and that, to me, is disgraceful. The old game, pre Super League, along with its traditions have been shelved away without a thought as the new wave of ideas and marketing overwhelmed the old game like a tidal wave. I agree that the former law makers and governors of the old game did 'miss the boat' regarding sponsorships and marketing and I agree that something drastic had to be done to the old game to keep it a viable enterprise. But the total overnight changes all but destroyed the old game and its most prised possession, its traditions. These traditions should have been written in stone, not by this writer attempting to maintain a vestige of tradition, but through regular contact with the old players, managers, coaches and administrators.

I hope you enjoy this look backwards and hope it provides a few insights on how we approached the game in those far off days. Some of the antics and tactics, although to some extent brutal, are viewed in a slightly more nostalgic mood. They were happy days when we played in the snow and cold of winter.

1

HOW THE GAME EVOLVED

This first chapter deals with the reasons rugby football league branched away from the family of the Rugby Football Union. Our beloved game of rugby league football was born of the desire of a few brave men to see fair play and introduce common sense values into the world of the old working classes. At the time 'Masters', the bosses, employed a draconian style of rule which stated that 'no work, no pay' was rigidly adhered to. Saturday was classed as a working day, 'Thou shall labour six days and rest on the Sabbath'. If a person from the working classes was lucky to be good enough to gain a place in one of the class conscious rugby union clubs in his area, then he would have to get permission from his Master to have Saturday afternoon off when playing at home and possibly the full day off if playing away. If the Master agreed, as he was usually on the committee of a local Union club, then the player lost either a full or half day's pay.

The game of rugby union particularly in the south was a rich man's hobby, a sports club that the sons of business men and university men joined both as a leisure break at the weekend and to meet old chums from school and business. Up north the game exploded into life as an outlet from the drudgery of a brutal working environment. Suddenly the international scene stopped being the domain of the mediocre talented rich, as an exciting bunch of tough northern working class players forced their way into the county and national sides. Gone were the landed gentry and the mill owners' sons, the Oxford and Cambridge graduates, the lawyers and the doctors. In came the mill workers, builders, teachers, farm workers, blacksmiths, the foundry men and the labourers and with them they brought an aspect to the game never seen before in this sport for gentlemen. They played to win. They won by playing within the rules—toughness and hardness in running and in the tackle were within the rules. Suddenly, like stars from the London stage, the northern players were idolised, yet the union hierarchy would not bend in their determination to maintain a ban on all payments involving time off work to play. The term 'broken time payments' came into being as the strong northern clubs' committees petitioned the London-based Rugby Football Union for permission to pay their players for time off work to play.

At a meeting of the RFU in London on 20 September 1893, two representatives from Yorkshire, Mr J.A. Millar and Mr M. Newsome, proposed that 'Players be allowed compensation for bona fide loss of time at work'. A total of 136 voted in favour but 282 voted against. Most (but not all) of the top Yorkshire and Lancashire clubs and one or two clubs from Cheshire discussed and supported the idea of paying broken time. The senior clubs, encouraged by the 136 votes for the proposal made at the RFU meeting, called a meeting on 29 August 1895 at the George Hotel, Huddersfield. Twenty-one northern senior club representatives attended this historic meeting, chaired by the powerful Mr H.H. [Harry] Waller of the Brighouse club. The chairman received motions and ideas from the members from the following clubs: Oldham, Halifax, Leeds, Bradford, Hull, Hunslet, Huddersfield, Wakefield, Widnes, Broughton Rangers, Batley, St Helens, Leigh, Warrington, Tyldesley, Wigan, Manningham, Rochdale Hornets, Dewsbury, Brighouse and

Liversedge. The clubs were asked to consider the proposals and vote. Dewsbury, after debate between their members present, withdrew. The tremendous step of resigning from the Rugby Football Union was taken and the brand new body of teams gloried in the title of the Northern Rugby Union which immediately declared that legitimate broken time expenses would be paid. The first steps to what would embrace in just over 100 years time, a full time game, the Super League, were taken. Rules, regulations and new by-laws were drawn up and it all began.

Whilst the broken time payments were an issue, other things drove the northern administrators to abandon their 'father' figure, the Rugby Football Union. The advent of professional soccer, particularly in the north of England, was seen as a threat but the governing body saw no problems with these professional 'bounders' and the continued, apparently flippant, attitudes of the Rugby Football Union rubbed like a sore on the heels of the northern clubs. Issues such as organised and regular week-by-week fixtures were considered unimportant by the RFU. It was thought at the time that when the governing body realised the implications of this determined effort by the northern clubs, the HQ in London would react favourably and agree to most of their suggestions. It had the reverse effect and the RFU warned the northern clubs that if they proceeded with broken time payments they would be thrown out of the RFU and deemed 'professional'.

The first fixture list of the fledgling league (as the Northern Union) played on 7 September 1895 under the RFU rules was:

Batley v Hull
Bradford v Wakfield Trinity
Broughton Rangers v Wigan
Leigh v Leeds
Liversedge v Halifax

> Runcorn v Widnes
> St Helens v Rochdale Hornets
> Stockport v Brighouse Rangers
> Tyldesley v Manningham
> Warrington v Hunslet
> (Huddersfield and Oldham did not play on the opening weekend.)

The RFU's reaction to this was to draw down an iron curtain immediately and forbid their remaining member clubs from playing with or against any team in the Northern Union. The existing rules regarding professionalism were extended to class any player found to be even training with the Northern Union as a professional and bar them from the RFU. Because the RFU lost almost its entire group of top northern players in one dramatic swoop, the fortunes of the England rugby union team dropped disastrously and they suffered a period of defeats never before experienced. For this reason, the RFU never forgave both the Northern Union or its later offshoot, the Rugby Football League and imposed the most stringent barriers against even amateur players who had played one game of rugby league after the age of 15 years old. The new union prospered and in 1897 the new idea of a Challenge Cup came to fruition and the clubs played for the Northern Union Challenge Cup. Batley and St Helens won their way through to the final at Headingley. Batley's 'Gallant Youths' won the cup with a score of 10–3 before a crowd of 14,000.

Mr Waller was in the chair again at the second annual general meeting when a further wedge was driven between the two handling codes. The value of a goal kick in the Northern Union was agreed to be two points for any type of goal kicked and a try would count as three points. The RFU still played to four points for a drop goal, three for a penalty and two for a conversion. The Northern Union abolished the line-out and replaced it with the rather scrappy kick-in or 'punt out' from touch. Mr Waller reported that 59 teams were members of the new union and it was necessary to split the teams into two leagues called the Yorkshire Senior Competition and the Lancashire Senior Competition. Inter county club games could be played with a shared gate but the results of these games would not count in the two leagues' points tally. The game was, although still played at 15 a side, drifting away from the mother game of rugby union. It was evolving into its own unique format. As the crowds warmed to this new and exciting game and bigger crowds began to appear at the ordinary league games, it was only natural that players looked towards a fully professional game. The meeting of 1898 accepted that the Northern Union would adopt a policy of professionalism. The meeting thrashed out a four point charter which stated:

1] That professionalism would be adopted
2] That players be properly registered with their club
3] That players must have legitimate employment in a full time job other than football and
4] That severe penalties would be imposed for offences against the mentioned conditions.

Legitimate employment did not include bookies runner, billiard marker or public house waiter. This meant some good players were suspended for not having a 'legitimate' job and unable to play until they found one meaning some clubs were in a mess. This stringent rule was known as the 'working clause' and various players fell foul of it. One player had his registration refused because he was a waiter in a local pub, another player took time off work to visit a sick relative and was stopped playing on a Saturday until the club received a note from his employer saying he was back at work. Dai

Fitzgerald, the strong running Batley centre and a cup final player, was suspended for two seasons until he found a full time job.

Teams from Cumberland, a hot bed of rugby men, Whitehaven, Maryport, Wath Brow and Seaton were admitted into the union and this was enough to allow Cumberland entry into the county championship. At the time of the union turning professional, its membership stood at 98 clubs. The season 1898–99 was the first full season of professionalism and more and more clubs opted for the freedom of the new Union. York, Featherstone, Normanton and Rothwell joined from the Yorkshire area and the Lancashire combination league had to be split into north Lancashire, south Lancashire and Cumberland sections because of the increase in new clubs joining the union.

The RFU contacted the two other unions, Wales and Scotland to be on their guard against the 'scouts' being sent to poach the good players into the Northern Union. Tales of scouts being attacked, beaten up and thrown into rivers or even the sea were enough to put off the usually doughty poachers from the north. Several stories have been handed down through the years about the treatment of scouts. One story from the borders of Scotland shows just how fervent the Scots were when it came to toeing the RFU line regarding the poaching of rugby union players. A scout had gone up to the borders to look at a superb centre and an alert ticket collector noticed that the traveller had a ticket from Leeds. 'Here for the big game are ye?' asked the collector.

'Er, no,' replied the scout and set off for the ground. On his arrival he found a body of local men barring his way. The local men quickly lifted him bodily and marched the short distance to the trout river and swung him out a few times by the arms and legs over the fast flowing water. Back on dry land they told him in no uncertain manner that if he returned to take players from Scotland then he would go into the river. The body of Scotsmen frog marched the scout back to the station and pushed him onto the train to Carlisle, whether or not he wanted to go to Carlisle.

Another legendary story is of the signing of an international Scots forward by the Wigan club whose representatives had crept into the town of Hawick to sign him. Such was the secrecy of the signing that it was concluded by candlelight in the hotel attic so that the dastardly deed was not discovered.

A few years ago, just before the RFU embraced professionalism themselves, I was at a rugby union game at a swish Yorkshire club and went in for a pint after the game. I noticed a large painting on the wall of a Yorkshire versus Lancashire county game played on the ground way back in 1898. Some of the players' faces had been obliterated by the rubbing of a thumb and I asked the club steward why the faces were missing. 'Oh, those are the ones who signed for the Northern Union,' he answered.

But most club scouts persevered with their trips down into Wales and up into Scotland, despite the tough provocation received in these two areas. Some unusual tales emerged from their efforts to poach players, particularly from the principality and bring them up north. The RFU had noted, as early as 1890, some northern clubs must be paying broken time payments and in 1892 the Broughton Rangers club from Manchester managed to bring two fantastic international players to the north from Swansea, the brothers Evan and Dai James. These brilliant half backs, it was published in a Swansea newspaper, moved up north because Swansea would not pay broken time. This action suggested that Broughton Rangers would pay broken time. The superb brothers were declared professionals in early 1893 but after repeated appeals from the Swansea club and supported by the Welsh rugby union, the brothers were, in an unbelievable about turn by the RFU secretary, G. Rowland Hill, awarded amateur reinstatement in 1896. The story did not end there as three years later, in 1899, not only did Evan and

Dai return to Manchester but with them came the whole family of 16 including brothers Sam, Will and Claude who all signed for Broughton Rangers. The interesting point is that Sam was 16 years of age, Will 14 years old and Claude was the ripe old age of 10. The outlay of cash for the five brothers was £200.

The sad thing was that almost all the players who signed for Northern Union clubs were suspended from the RFU for life and in some cases not allowed in the pubs from where teams were run. Despite the upset the breakaway caused there are some funny tales that hang over from those far off days. The author's adopted home town of Morley is now a suburb of the sprawling Leeds City. In 1895 however Morley was a borough in its own right and had a successful, tough rugby union side. Morley business men gained their wealth mainly from the shoddy wool trade and from such unusual trades as rhubarb growing. But the club had well off patrons and on the fateful day on 29 August 1895 the Morley club were invited to the meeting at the George Hotel. The mode of transport back then was the horse and trap, carriages were for the real toffs, and the Morley club secretary and the vice chairman set off from Scatchard Lane early in the trap. The secretary headed for Huddersfield and travelled via the top road in Cleckheaton where the two famous pubs stand, the Old Pack Horse and the New Pack Horse. Being a wee bit early the two men called in for a 'quick one' at 9.30am and emerged at 4.30pm. This was why Morley did not join the breakaway.

The second Challenge Cup final was again played at Headingley with the attendance doubling to a mighty 27,941. The strong Batley side retained the cup by way of a 7–0 win over Bradford. The teams in that final were, Batley: Garner; 'Wattie' Davies, Fitzgerald, J.B. Goodall, Fozzard; Oakland, H. Goodall; Shackleton, Jim Gath, Maine, Spurr, Fisher, Stubley, Munns and Rodgers. The Bradford side were: Patrick; Cooper, W. Murgatroyd, F. Murgatroyd, Dodson; Wood, Prole; Broadley, McLoughlin, Toothill, Fearnley, Holt,

Holden, Robertson and Kelsey. Batley's scores were J.B. Goodall try and one drop goal, 'Wattie' Davies one drop goal.

The year 1902 saw a major change to the rules of the still fledgling game when kicks into touch without a bounce were only allowed to make ground from a penalty kick. Field kicks made to gain ground had to bounce in the field of play before crossing the touchline. The RFU rules still allowed a kick to go out of play on the full and make ground on any kick taken. This change brought about more short tactical kicking, especially the grubber kick, much favoured by a scrum half running to the 'blind side', or short side of a scrum and hitting a 20 yard grubber kick up field into touch. He then trusted his forwards to win the ball back in the tight scrum. Playing behind a good pack of forwards, a scrum half could gain many valuable yards in a game with this ploy.

Arguably the most prestigious change in the new game's laws was the one that totally divided the two handling codes when, in the 1906–07 season, the Northern Union dropped the number of men per team to 13. The format of the sides meant the two wing forwards were redundant, making a Northern Union pack of forwards six in number. This totally distinguished the game from that of the RFU. Just one other fundamental and vital change had taken place in 1899 to tidy up the game and make it presentable to the ever growing number supporters of the professional code. Alas this particular change took many years of tinkering and new ideas before a successful style evolved. This was the way that the ball was brought back into play after a tackle, the play the ball. Initially the ruling of bringing the ball back into play was the same as the RFU. But the new think tank considered this too time consuming as too many rucks and mauls developed at every tackle. So when a player and ball were 'held' in the tackle a scrum was formed. If the player or ball were not held the player could pass it or drop it to the ground provided the ball did not drop in a forward direction and play continued. The answer was obvious but it was not until a few years later that today's play the ball [still with its frailties] evolved.

The other acceptable change at the 1899 meeting concerned restarting play after a try was scored. Up to this change of rule, the defending side kicked off from its own '25' yard line. This was sensibly changed to kick off from the half way line. Another change to the kicking game was also agreed. In the RFU a player could catch a ball on the full, with both feet on the ground, from an opponent's kick and on the point of catching the ball, dig his heel in the ground and call, 'Mark!' This allowed the catcher a 'free kick', either down field, into touch or even a kick at goal. The kick at goal was abolished from a mark in 1922 but a returned kick down field or into touch was retained. The mark to this day is still allowed in the RFU.

Many aspects of the modern game have evolved into things that our grandfathers would not recognise if they could return to witness today's game. The organised scrum has manifested from a mass of players rucking and mauling for the ball on the ground, a little reminiscent of the Eton Wall game, where a melee of a seemingly pointless, unmoving mass of bodies, striving to uncover and move a ball never seen beneath the bodies, into a fairly neat formation of six forwards each. Under today's uncompetitive rules they can do very little wrong in bringing the ball back into play. Not so in grandad's day, goodness me no, as we will discuss later. We have moulded our initial game into a contest now manufactured for the vast TV audience. There is no doubt at all that there has been progress but at a huge cost to old established principles that were forged back in 1895 and, of course, before that when we played under the auspices of the RFU.

Not all supporters are totally sold on this modern concept, many favour the winter bite of cool, fresh weekends with games played in a climate for which the game was originally planned but, as with most things and as things happened in 1895, the game will be played as dictated by the clubs' leaders. To cover every reason for change and each decision made way back at that immense meeting at the George Hotel in Huddersfield in 1895, would take a book thicker than Tolstoy's *War and Peace*. I have covered, in this lesser book, the areas that produced the game we love today. I earnestly believe that the tradition built in our game, over the 100 odd years before Super League, was the catalyst from which our modern league sprang. Make no mistake, the Rugby Football League was no easy land full of milk and honey. Many clubs struggled financially for years simply to keep going. For a club in membership of the Rugby Football League, that club was the focus for lots of supporters from the surrounding community. The link between the supporters and the parent club was as fervent as any feeling that a soccer follower has for Manchester United or Liverpool. In fact in most cases, because of the game's northern roots and its minority crowds compared to first division soccer, the feeling was more fervent.

Obviously, one's school and parents had a big effect on the sport one followed. In the average working class northern towns, schools played rugby league as opposed to rugby union but soccer always seemed to be a favourite of teachers in charge of sport. This was possibly because soccer was easier to play in my day. It could be played on a cinder pitch as opposed to rugby which required a field. Simple games, imitating the main game, such as 'shots in' could be played with a goal chalked on a wall and one or two defending whilst one or two attacked. Rugby league was far more difficult to organise. Hence the teachers who insisted on their school playing rugby league were like the Apostles of the Christian faith, they sought converts. The teachers were fired up by the whole concept of the game, its character building properties of giving and taking a knock without complaint left those not too well off kids with a winning attitude to face the world. The game that evolved into the show piece it is today started with these vital principles of 'play as hard as you can but play fair'.

The general meeting of the Northern Union clubs for the 1899–1900 season was filled with various motions to change some of the laws still attached to the RFU and its laws of the game. The knock on law was still the same as the RFU. If a player fumbled the catch of either a kick, pick up or pass, it was deemed to be a knock on. A proposal to make the existing rule less harsh, allowing a player to juggle with the ball and retain possession so long as the ball did not touch the ground, was defeated. The Northern Union had introduced a law on new amendments or anything to change the game's format which meant that to win the amendment, a vote of three fourths must be in favour. The vote concerning the knock on supported the change but did not have the three fourths majority. It was the same in the case of a proposed scrum instead of the hated punt out from touch to restart play. One law that was changed was to ban the opposing team charging at a goal kicker after a try. The team having the try scored against them had to stand still over their own goal line in the field of play, between their try line and dead ball line, until the kick had been taken. A final new rule was that a limit of 75 players was placed on every club. This ruling stopped certain clubs from 'hording' players, as one club in particular had over 200 players on its books. Some of the more wealthy clubs were tired of being stopped by the votes of the 'lesser' clubs as the leading clubs wanted the changes in ruling.

The idea of a 'super league' was suggested at the 1898–99 general meeting but was not granted a second thought. Those clubs who were well supported and well housed in nice grounds with good sides, worked secretly together and called a meeting. Twelve club representatives collected in Huddersfield in the summer of 1901 and drew up the plans for a Northern League of which there would be 12 clubs, Batley, Broughton Rangers, Bradford, Halifax,

Huddersfield, Hull, Hunslet, Runcorn, Salford, Oldham, Swinton and Warrington (six clubs apiece from Lancashire and Yorkshire). The idea of the inter county club games was thought to be the answer to the ordinary local fixtures of the Yorkshire and Lancashire Senior Competitions which were becoming a little stale. The flag ship league was launched in May 1901. Arguments started immediately as several clubs thought that they had as much to offer as any of the founder members of this new born Northern Rugby League. There were howls of derision as the smaller clubs relied on the bigger teams visiting their grounds for the rich gates they brought. The meeting of the newly formed management committee in June 1901 developed into a hard talking debate and with the lucky 12 banding together they won the day on a 12 to 11 vote (a majority of one!) Meanwhile the still operating Northern Union continued with its accepted competitions with Oldham winning the Lancashire Senior Competition and Bradford winning the Yorkshire Championship. Batley, the 'Gallant Youths' as they became known, again won the Challenge Cup, beating Warrington at Headingley by 6–0 before 30,000 folk.

Due to pressure from the remainder of the Northern Union, the new league was increased by two, Brighouse Rangers and Leigh. As a compromise it was agreed that the bottom team in the Northern League would be relegated and a play off between the winners of the Yorkshire and Lancashire Senior Competitions would decide the promoted team. The teams in the Yorkshire competition felt let down by the secrecy of the formulation of the Northern League and boycotted fixtures with the elite 14. The Yorkshire Senior Competition, determined to maintain a competition without the Northern Leaguers, invited some of the junior teams in the county to join their competition and formed a 14 strong league. The full league was made up of Bramley, Keighley, Manningham, Heckmondwike, Leeds, Wakefield Trinity, York, Castleford, Liversedge, Goole,

Dewsbury, Sowerby Bridge, Holbeck and Normanton.

The Lancashire clubs carried out a more sensible plan by opting to play some of the Northern League teams in a South West and South East competition and invite a few successful junior sides to join them. The Lancashire Senior outfit also accepted into their league a very unusual applicant, Hull Kingston Rovers, who, it was said, were sick and tired of the Yorkshire Seniors' attitude to an elite league. The huge problem arose over the transferring of players from the Yorkshire Senior Competition to the Northern League. The Lancashire men had agreed a system of transfers with the Northern League that were agreeable to them and the ultra strained feeling between the Northern League teams and the Yorkies continued throughout the season 1901–02.

The laws were altered as the suggested knock on ruling was accepted and the dreaded punt out was amended so that if the ball was carried out of play over the touchline, then a scrum would bring it back into play, if kicked out then the punt out was retained. The close season of 1901–02 saw the demise of two clubs but the introduction of a new club, South Shields from County Durham. The Leeds Parish Church club and founder member, Tyldesley, both withdrew because of the loss of their grounds. This traumatic and upsetting season ended with a magnificent Challenge Cup win for Broughton Rangers against Salford at Rochdale Hornets ground by 25–0 before a disappointing crowd of 15,000.

The general meeting in the summer of 1902 finally abolished the punt out rule, and introduced a 10 yard scrum from the touchline, in line with where the ball crossed the touchline. The formulation of a second division was also brought into operation with a 12 team league initially extended to an 18 team league. The first division was also extended to 18 clubs with the promotion of Wigan, Widnes, Hull Kingston Rovers and St Helens. The Leeds club missed out despite a runaway success in the Yorkshire Senior Competition championship the previous season and a first class ground and had to be satisfied with a place in the newly formed division two. This division included some strange names when we look at today's league set up but it also contained some well known clubs too. The division was made up of Birkenhead Wanderers, Millom, South Shields, Stockport, Dewsbury, York, Keighley, Barrow, Castleford, Manningham, Bramley, Normanton, Rochdale Hornets, Holbeck, Wakefield Trinity, Lancaster, Leeds and Morecambe. Halifax and Salford reached the final of the Challenge Cup which was played at Headingley and saw Halifax the winners in a 7–0 dreary type of match. On Saturday 25 April 1903, over 32,500 spectators witnessed the final proving, once again, that the Leeds ground was one of the best in the game. In that first two division season, as expected, the newly promoted clubs, Wigan, Widnes, Saints and Hull Kingston Rovers, along with the struggling Brighouse Rangers all finished at the foot of the league table, whilst in division two, Keighley were champions at the top of the league and Leeds were the runners up.

The rather dull final brought about another cry for the reduction of players per team. There was also the fear, amongst the league's various committees, for the general financial welfare of several clubs in the second division. Successful clubs were under pressure as their players asked for more money as the first division teams drew in decent crowds. Some sceptics wondered if moving away from the financial comfort of the RFU had been worthwhile. But the game went on. St Helens and Brighouse Rangers were relegated for the season 1903–04 whilst Leeds and Keighley were promoted. The sad thing was that the grand old Manningham club and the Stockport team went out of existence. This brought home to many of the remaining clubs the need for stringent housekeeping. Pontefract came into the second division. South Shields lasted only one season before being voted out of division two as Halifax again lifted the Challenge Cup after beating Warrington by 8–3 at Salford with a disappointing 17,041 people watching. There was an unusual occurrence at Dewsbury during the season. The area around Dewsbury underwent a scare as smallpox was thought to be rife in the town. Teams refused point blank to play at Crown Flatt until the area was deemed safe. An immense backlog of fixtures built up but, as the fear eased, the Dewsbury club fulfilled all their fixtures and won the second division championship to boot in a wonderful performance. As most second division clubs struggled financially it was no surprise that the Cheshire-based Birkenhead Wanderers retired just over half way through the season.

Warrington fought their way to consecutive finals when they took on Hull Kingston Rovers once again at Headingley. The 'Wire' registered a 6–0 victory over the game East Hull outfit in front of an acceptable crowd of almost 20,000. The ill-fated two divisions were abolished at the 1905 general meeting as was the despised and almost impossible to legislate 'working clause'. This made various club secretaries' jobs much easier but caused one or two cries of derision as the fears that the top stars would demand more money and thus, without having a full time job away from football, become full time professionals. Without realising it the brave and superbly old fashioned gentlemen who created the rugby league game had moulded a sport that, by its own appeal and quality, had to become a full time professional sport sooner or later. This happened much later of course through simple evolvement and the sport became Super League. As in most new ventures there were casualties amongst the clubs and the weakest went to the wall. The five counties playing and forming a strong inter county competition in 1903–04 reduced to three, Lancashire, Cumberland and Yorkshire, these counties playing a three team county championship. The two grand old cups, the Lancashire and Yorkshire cups were introduced to add a touch of extra competition and these became a firm favourite amongst fans and were massively important cups for players to win.

The 1905–06 season, played in one huge league with fixtures arranged between individual clubs, was not a success. It was obvious that some crucial change had to be made to support and bolster waning interests. One huge step was taken in 1906 when the Huddersfield club paid five golden sovereigns to sign for life the most famous player in the history of our game. He was signed whilst playing for Underbank Rangers in the Bradford and District league and his name was Harold Wagstaff. The player was known worldwide by a very apt nickname, 'The Prince of Centres'. Wagstaff was 15 years old when he made his debut for Huddersfield at the Barley Mow, Bramley and scored a try in the second half. He went on to captain his county, his club side which was the best team ever seen in its day and called 'Huddersfield, the Team of All Talents' and his country. He was a fantastic player who not only scored tries for himself but made try scoring easy for his wingman. His long time wing partner, Stanley Moorhouse scored many memorable tries, mostly from Wagstaff's passes and always said that his success was down to having Harold Wagstaff as his centre.

For the 1906–07 season teams were reduced to 13 a side. Through law and rule changes the old game started evolving into the game of today. The play the ball was, after a few more years, ironed out into something acceptable and our beloved game was up and running. All we needed was the extra spice of overseas opponents. This was catered for in 1907–08 in the shape of a mostly New Zealand team, with a smattering of extremely talented Australians and managed by a smart New Zealander and entrepreneur A.H. Baskerville and his team nicknamed, 'Baskervilles All Golds'. This tour is described in more detail in *chapter 3, Aussie, Kiwi and Springbok Players*. Four current 'All Blacks' were with this touring side, W.H. Mackrell, D. McGregor, George Smith and W. Johnston and the Aussie, the 'master' H.H.

'Dally' Messenger and Kiwi Lance. B. Todd. Dally Messenger became the greatest star player and centre ever produced by Australia, possibly bigger than Reg Gasnier or Andrew 'Joey' Johns and the prestigious 'Dally M' medal is presented annually to the best young player in Australia. Lancelot Beaumont Todd came over to play at stand off half for Wigan and became a great and successful broadcaster and administrator in the game over here. The Lance Todd Trophy, given to the outstanding player in the Challenge cup final is named in his honour. Baskerville's team aroused immense interest and played their first ever 13 a side game in this country against Bramley at the old Barley Mow ground, a game the tourists won with ease. Representative games were played against the tourists at Cheltenham and Stamford Bridge, Chelsea and a third was played at Headingley. These three games were called 'Test Matches' after the international cricket games and the title stuck.

Twelve months after Baskerville's team departed back home the first official Northern Union tour by the Australian national team took place. This was brought about because during the successful Baskerville tour of England, the New South Wales rugby union, whose players had suffered under the 'no broken time' rule down under, met and decided to inspect the Northern Union rules, accept them and organise a tour of England sailing in the summer of 1908. On their way home to New Zealand, Baskerville's team played three games in Australia under Northern Union rules and New South Wales officially broke away from the Australian rugby union to adopt the new rules of rugby football. The secretary of the new Aussie game was Mr J.J. Giltinan whose name graces the J.J. Giltinan Shield still played today. An interesting fact of this inaugural tour was that one of the hookers, Sid 'Sandy' Pearce of Eastern Suburbs also came as a 41 years old player on the 1921–22 tour, some 13 years after the first tour and played 32 games in 1908 and 21 games in 1922.

So the old lady, our game, lurched on through great national depressions when it became the only thing, sometimes, that offered an outlet for one's frustrations. It was there to greet warriors returning home from the war on more than one occasion after years away. It eased the soldiers back into civilian lifestyle. The enemy in the Second World War, in occupied France, banned the game and the Vichy government confiscated all its assets, including its money, but still it survived.

As you read farther into this book it will give, to those who were not around then and to some who were, an insight as to what happened behind the scenes. It will also describe what happened on the field and what made the game tick in those far off days when our dad was a hero to most and our mam was an angel in a 'pinny' and looked after us so well. Enjoy the journey into *One Hundred Winters*, it tells how it was then.

2

WELSH PLAYERS

How can one describe the players in professional rugby league from the concept of the breakaway in 1895 to the formulation of Super League? At first, the game was only a part time profession played solely in the industrial north and in a smattering of clubs in South Wales over the years. Most players held down a day time job and were usually employed in physical work. The Yorkshire and Lancashire coalfield areas bred an untold number of top players, as did the mines of Cumberland where many miners worked the seams of coal miles out under the Irish Sea. Foundry workers, welders, the building industry, brick makers, painters and decorators and general labourers were the hard working men who turned out for training, as it was known then, in all sorts of weather when, if sane, they would have been in their homes in front of a cosy coal fire. When remembering that the game was played throughout the winter season, the idea of going out into the darkness, in wind, snow, rain and hail to a training session after a hard day's graft, speaks volumes about the players' dedication to their chosen sport. They trained on icy surfaces, in sodden canvas training footwear and, at the absolute limit of boredom, running up and down the steep terraces of the grandstand for what seemed like an eternity (the coach said it built 'stamina').

The major reason the players got through the months of almost unacceptable training was due to the comradeship of their team mates and the tremendous humour generated by the hundreds of natural comics who attended every single club in the league. High spirited jokes were worked at some time or other on every player. The communal bath after training and games was usually the focal point. That was when the relaxing players were most vulnerable. The old bucket of icy water, thrown over the dreamy players as they sat in the warm, balmy, soothing bath waters always brought about shrieks of anguish from the unsuspecting bathers and retribution was usually taken against the bucket thrower. Sometimes a shoe or a shirt would suddenly appear in the bath as an invisible thrower would deposit the item into the water. The unfortunate player at the butt end of the humour always gained his revenge before the end of the season. But for all the 'nobble' and mickey taking, when push came to shove in the heat of the battle on the Saturday afternoon, the icy water thrower or the invisible clothes chucker would be first to stand by any mate in trouble.

Of course almost all the players had different temperaments and the dressing room was cosmopolitan. Local dialects included the unmistakable Humberside drawl, with the 'farve' for five and the 'narn' for nine, the 'thees' and 'thars' of the Castleford and Featherstone areas, the accentuated 'Whoos' and growling 'r's' from our Lancastrian mates and that almost mystic Cumbrian accent that becomes inaudible when spoken quickly. Whilst manual workers formed the bulk of rugby league teams, there were players from other types of employment. Quite a few school teachers, a few university lecturers, bank clerks, shop and store workers, students, and a few, but not many, pure academics were involved in teams. There were other accents too. Almost every side in the Rugby Football League and the Northern Union before that, had at least one Welshman in their squad—more sometimes—the odd Scot and, very rarely, an Irishman. Wales of course had a strong national side in the old European Championship competition. In fact from the first 'Test' match against the Northern Union in 1908 there had been at least one Welshman in our international side right through to when the great hooker, Tommy Harris, pulled out of the first Test in New Zealand on the 1958 tour down under through injury. He was back for the second Test but unfortunately the link was broken but it was testimony to the strength of the Welshmen who came north that the inclusion of men from the principality, for just over 50 years, showed how important those Welsh signings were.

To name all the Welsh players who took the professional ticket would be impossible and to name all the players from Wales who were brilliant footballers would fill many books. So as we take this stroll through the game that was so different from the game we watch and play today, those who are too young to remember some of the players mentioned must make do with the memories that we old timers love to reminisce on.

Going back to the breakaway, one of the original successful sides, Batley, realised early on the worth of good Welsh players and Dai Fitzgerald joined the Gallant Youths after a spell at Leigh. A friend of Fitzgerald in Cardiff expressed a desire also to play at Batley and he duly arrived. Wharton Peers Davies was his name and he stayed at Mount Pleasant from 1896 to 1912. 'Wattie' Davies was a tremendous goal kicker and a prolific try scorer. The excellent centre Bert Jenkins of Wigan made two tours, the first in 1910 under the first tour captain, Jim Lomas of Salford with fellow Welshman, Cliff. Jenkins [Ebbw Vale], Johnny Thomas [Wigan], Jim Davies [Huddersfield], George Ruddick [Broughton Rangers], Frank Shugars [Warrington] and Frank 'Bucket' Young [Leeds] were the other Welsh players in the team. The second was in 1914 with the great Harold Wagstaff as skipper along with the Welsh contingent of Jack Chilcott [Huddersfield], Percy Coldrick [Wigan], Alf Francis [Hull], Bert Jenkins [Wigan], W.A. 'Willie' Davies [Leeds], Stuart

Prosser [Halifax], Johnny Rogers [Huddersfield], Gwyn Thomas [Wigan] and Frank Williams [Halifax]. On the 1920 tour no fewer than eight men from the principality were selected with Wagstaff as captain again. The players were Jim Bacon [Leeds], Evan Davies [Oldham], Ben Gronow [Huddersfield], Danny Hurcombe [Wigan], Robbie Lloyd [Halifax], George Rees [Leeds], Johnny Rogers [Huddersfield] and Gwyn Thomas [Huddersfield]. The great Ben Gronow was named 'unknown' in a team picture of a Yorkshire Cup winning team when he was coach of the club. The picture appeared in the *Morley Rugby Union Centenary* brochure and was a show of disrespect by Northern Union men some 70 years after the split. Ben Gronow had kicked off in the first game at Twickenham for Wales against England at rugby union and played in seven Test matches for the Great Britain team as well as gaining that full international status for Wales at rugby union.

Among the lists of the many great world class players who came north was a youngster at the tender age of 17 years old. His rugby union club was Cardiff and his name was Jim Sullivan. Jim was a big man in every sense of the word, big in physique, big in ability and big in character. He was, on the whole, a one club man (apart from 31 games played for three clubs, Dewsbury (27), Keighley (3) and Bradford Northern (1) as a guest player in war time football) and was true to the club who had brought him north, Wigan. He signed for Wigan in June 1921: he played his first game for them in August 1921 and his final game for them in February 1946. His career included 928 first class games, 774 of them for Wigan and he kicked an unbelievable 2,867 goals, scoring 96 tries for a career total of 6,022 points. He made three tours, 1924, 1928 and captained the 1932 tourists. 'Peerless Jim' was indeed a Welsh jewel.

At the annual meeting of 1922, two vital amendments were made: the parochial name of the Northern Union was abolished and the title Rugby League was instituted; and being allowed to kick at goal from a mark was struck from the laws of the game. By the tour of 1924 the Welsh players in the game had now become the backbone of our international and local league sides. Jonty Parkin [Wakefield Trinity] had taken over the captaincy of the tourists from the great Harold Wagstaff and this tour would also see the introduction of two Welsh players who would hold records in the game for many years. Jim Sullivan [Wigan] and Joe Thompson [Leeds] would both make three consecutive tours, a marvellous achievement. The Welsh contingent on this tour included, Jim Bacon [Leeds], Frank Evans [Swinton], Ben Gronow [Huddersfield], Danny Hurcombe [Wigan], Tommy Howley [Wigan], Dai Rees [Halifax] and Johnny Ring [Wigan].

Of the 13 players who constitute the Rugby League Hall of Fame, three are Welshmen. These players are Jim Sullivan, Gus Risman and the great Billy Boston. All three were backs, which belies the quality of Welsh forwards who changed codes over the years. Sullivan's and Risman's careers overlapped but Boston came later. In the early days of the game, arguably the biggest stars in the breakaway game were Billy Batten, born in Kinsley, a small mining village near Hemsworth on 26 May 1889 in the West Riding of Yorkshire and of course the legendary Harold Wagstaff. But the principality supplied excellent players throughout the Northern Union as the broken time ban by the strict RFU ruling was not as strongly enforced in the northern counties. Many Welsh players found their way up north well before the breakaway. Almost every side had a Williams, Jones, Thomas, Jenkins, Hughes, Evans, Rees, Watkins, Davies, James or a Bevan amongst their players. The word was spread when a northern team toured South Wales that such and such a team paid broken time and the cracking Welsh players, who then were 'whiter than white' regarding amateurism, would apply for a trial up north. Sometimes a scout would ask the players if they would like to trial with 'the' club and, if successful, would land a job and receive broken time payments. This made them much better off financially than they had been in Wales.

Some clubs had a leaning to sign Welsh players and usually had a secretive but excellent scouting system entrenched in the valleys and in the bigger cities such as Cardiff and Swansea, reminiscent of the spy network employed in both World Wars. Leeds always had good Welshmen on their books, as did Halifax and Salford. One of the first men from the valleys to sign for Leeds was the strong and speedy centre, Tommy Llewellyn, who registered 53 tries in 158 games around the turn of the century and two other top Welsh try scorers, J.P. Jenkins and W. Evans ably abetting him. Later the free scoring W.D. Llewellyn and Phil Thomas joined the club. Some of the Welsh players who graced the blue and amber jersey of Leeds before the start of hostilities in 1939 included Evan Williams, Joe Thompson, Billy Bowen, Jim Bacon, Billy Lyons [the last four all came from the Cross Keys club], Mel Rosser, Dan Pascoe, Arthur 'Candy' Evans bought from Halifax, George Andrews, Cliff Evans, Dicky Ralph, Gwyn Parker, Aubrey Casewell, Iowerth Isaac. The brilliant Oliver Morris, signed from Hunslet and so tragically killed in Italy serving as an officer during the Second World War, should not be forgotten. The superb pairing at Swinton of that terrific half back duo, Bryn Evans (English although of Welsh ancestry) and 'Billo' Rees on the 1928 tour, skippered for the second time by the outstanding Jonty Parkin [Wakefield Trinity] also included Welshmen Joe Thompson [Leeds], Mel Rosser [Leeds], Emlyn Gwynne [Hull], Jim Sullivan [Wigan] and Billy Williams [Salford]. The Welsh stars who made the 1932 tour under Jim Sullivan's captaincy, Gus Risman [Salford], Joe Thompson [Leeds], Ivor Davies [Halifax], Billy Williams [Salford], Les White [Hunslet] and Norman Fender [York] all contributed highly to a successful winning tour in both countries down under.

There were of course many other fine Welsh players who for one reason or another never made the touring teams. I illustrate the Welsh tourists because the honour of tour selection was the highest accolade the one could achieve in those days and of course to mention every great Welsh player would fill a hundred books. Jim Brough [Leeds], a Cumberland fisherman whom Leeds signed from Liverpool FC at Anfield, was the captain of the 1936 tour. This was after the great man, Jim Sullivan, chosen as captain to make his fourth tour, withdrew because of a family illness. The Welshmen under Jim Brough on that trip were the dynamic Salford pair of half backs, Emlyn Jenkins and Billy Watkins. From Wigan came the classical centre Gwyn Davies, the flying dentist from Newport, wingman Jack Morley and Keighley's Hal Jones. The baby of the party was the excellent Salford finisher, Alan Edwards, a scorer of 21 tries on that tour. The brilliant Gus Risman of Salford was also included on the tour making the second of his three tours. In three of the five test matches on the 1936 tour, Salford provided five of the backs, four of them Welshmen, Risman, Edwards, Barney Hudson from Durham, Jenkins and Watkins. The 1940 tour was postponed because of the war and the interruption of the 10 years between tours cost many good Welsh players a tour place. Many Welsh players provided entertainment for our beleaguered country when, as servicemen, they played as guest players for other clubs in the war time league.

The immediate post war era witnessed many Welsh players taking the trip north. The Welsh national team was included in the European Championship competition which comprised at one period, England, France, Wales and the Other Nationalities and was played on a league basis. The war took away the best years in several players' careers but one outstanding forward from Wales played before, during and after the war, the majestic Trevor Foster of Bradford Northern, Wales and Great Britain. A magnificent sportsman and gentleman, Trevor was a prolific try scorer, which was unusual for a second row forward. Gus Risman continued to bring enjoyment to all who witnessed his performances as did the policeman, Arthur Bassett of Halifax. The 1947 Wembley Challenge Cup final between Bradford Northern and Leeds made a statement as to the strength and quality of the Welsh players in the game when 13 of the 26 players on duty were from the principality. Leeds had eight, Tommy Cornelius, Gareth Price, T.L. [Les] Williams, Dickie Williams, Dai Jenkins, Dai Prosser, Con Murphy and the fabulous Ike Owens. Bradford, the winners on the day by 8–4, fielded Emlyn Walters, the wonderful stand off W.T.H. [Willie] Davies from the fishing village of Penclawdd on the Gower coast, the huge Frank Whitcombe at field side prop, Trevor Foster, and the tough Hagan Evans at loose forward.

The first tour after the war in 1946, with the squad travelling to Australia on the aircraft carrier, HMS Indomitable, included 11 Welsh players, Joe Jones [Barrow], Ted Ward [Wigan], Trevor Foster [Bradford Northern], Ike Owens [Leeds], Doug Phillips [Oldham], Gus Risman [Salford], Frank Whitcombe [Bradford Northern], W.F. [Fred] Hughes [Workington Town] the father of Emlyn Hughes of Liverpool FC and England fame, Arthur Bassett [Halifax], Willie Davies [Bradford Northern] and Dai Jenkins [Leeds]. Doug Phillips had several mighty confrontations in the State and Test matches with the great Arthur Clues [Australia] and Ike Owens was rated the finest loose forward ever seen in Australia on that tour. That excellent three quarter Roy Francis [Wigan and Barrow], who hailed from Brynmawr and later became a superb coach at Hull FC and at Headingley, was an unlucky Welshman in that he gained only one international cap for Great Britain against New Zealand in 1947. Gareth Price was unfortunate never to gain full Great Britain selection as he was an outstanding centre for many seasons appearing at Wembley for Leeds and Halifax.

About this time, so the story goes at Headingley, the chairman and assistant secretary set off for the valleys to sign a stand off half who had been strongly recommended 12 months earlier by the Leeds club's chief scout in South Wales. They were deep in one of the Rhondda valleys and came across the mining village, described by the scout, where the stand off half lived. They pulled up in the car outside of the house and knocked on the door. It was around midday and a voice came from within the small back-to-back colliery house in answer to the knock, 'Come in please!' The voice had that delightful Welsh lilt. Inside the living room sat a well built young man, just about to tuck into his midday meal.

'We're from Leeds Rugby League Club and want to sign you on as a Leeds player. We're prepared to offer you £4,000 if you'll sign now,' and the chairman placed a small brief case on the table which contained the said amount in cash.

The young man wiped his mouth with a napkin and looked at the money, 'Oh no sir, you don't want to sign me', he said politely. The chairman would not let go as he saw a great stand off sat there and could see in his mind's eye the crowd cheering in ecstasy as this young Welsh athlete replaced a recent hero who had returned to Australia. 'No sir, you really don't want me,' the young man said again but the chairman thrust a registration form in front of him and held out a pen.

'Sign there,' he said pointing at the dotted line.

'Well if you insist,' the young Welshman said and signed.

'Thank you and this is now yours,' the chairman said sliding the briefcase over to the lad.

The lad took out the money, snapped the case closed, put the case behind him and stood up. Reaching for a pair of crutches, which were laid on the floor, he hitched himself up and explained. 'The money will come in useful, you see I had my leg amputated in an accident down the pit two months ago.' The former stand off star opened the door for the bemused Leeds officials and said, 'Goodbye gentlemen.' I have it from the assistant secretary that the story is true! You can please yourself whether you believe it or not but strange things do happen in those valleys!

Many more Welshmen were easily good enough to play for Great Britain but were around when there were several great players for each position then, George Parsons [Saints], Les Williams [Hunslet], Bryn Goldswain [Oldham], Billy Banks [Huddersfield], Mel Meek [Huddersfield], Con Murphy [Leeds] to name but a few. Halifax loved Welsh wingmen. Apart from Arthur Bassett they had Jim Bevan from Aberavon, Arthur Daniels, Dai Bevan, Terry Cook and the great Johnny Freeman. Leeds, Salford and Barrow brought arguably the three biggest signings north. The superb Lewis Jones came to Headingley in 1952 and the great David 'Dai' Watkins, of the famous smack in the mouth and the greeting, 'Welcome to rugby league,' joined Salford in 1967 from Newport. The unfortunate Keith Jarrett signed as an 18 year old 'wonder boy' for Barrow in 1969, again from Newport, but suffered a stroke and retired from the game at the unbelievably young age of 24. Saints had their share of very good 'converts' when they signed Kel Coslett, John Mantle, Bob Prosser, John Warlow and a little later the Llanelli and Wales full back, Clive Griffiths. Cardiff's international wingman, John Bevan signed, very successfully, for Warrington. The team also gained the services of the tough forward Bobby Wanbon. The illustrious list of great Welsh players goes on and it would be unfair not to mention the exciting runner Maurice Richards [Salford], the immortal Tommy Harris [Hull], the one and only Clive Sullivan [Hull FC and Hull Kingston Rovers], the great giant Jim Mills [Widnes], the granite tough Tony Fisher [Bradford Northern, Leeds and Castleford] and the superb Colin Dixon [Halifax and Salford]. I salute sincerely all the hundreds of great Welsh rugby players that I have not mentioned who came north.

3

AUSSIE, KIWI AND SPRINGBOK PLAYERS

Like the Welsh converts, Australians and New Zealanders took to the Northern Union concept like ducks to water. The freedom to run with the ball suited their strong and adventurous nature plus the broken time payments helped them adjust. The first move towards the Northern Union was made by the predominantly Kiwi tour of 1907. Landing in Folkstone on 30 September 1907 the 'All Gold's', as they were known because they were being paid expenses, included a famous Australian rugby union player, H.H. 'Dally' Messenger, who was supposed to be just about the best player of his generation. The tourists were part of what became known as 'Baskerville's tour', named after A.H. Baskerville of Wellington, one of the prime organisers of the trip. The chairman of the Northern Union Council, Mr H. Ashton of Warrington, told of how delighted the Northern Union were to welcome the pioneer visitors. The expenses the All Gold's received were paid out of the tourists' share of gate money after each game. The tourists played 35 games in all, winning 19. In winning two out of three tests they were able to break even financially. This tour not only opened doors for further tours, it also began the movement of players from down under coming to play for English clubs. Two top players of Baskerville's tour declared their intention of playing for Northern Union clubs, George Smith, an established All Black centre or wingman, although aged 35, had signed for Oldham. Wigan had swooped for a real bargain as they announced the signing of the talented stand off half, Lance B. Todd who went on to be an outstanding player, commentator and administrator in his long career in this country.

In 1908 New South Wales declared that they were embracing the Northern Union game and 12 months after Baskerville's tour, the first Australian tourists set sail for England aboard the HMS Macedonia. Amongst them were two priceless jewels, H.H. Dally Messenger and Albert Aaron Rosenfeld. The Aussie tour manager was the astute and streetwise Mr J.J. [James] Giltinan, who was also the secretary of the former New South Wales rugby union and a leading figure in the change to Northern Union rules. The first Australian tour captain was the North Sydney player, Dennis Lutge with Dally Messenger as vice-captain. The tourists travelled second class on a one way ticket and the return fare was to be paid out of the profits, if any, of the tour's share of gate money. James Giltinan was the man who coined the name the 'Kangaroo's' instead of the expected name the 'All Blues', as the tourists intended to play in sky blue jerseys. The tour began in September 1908 and ended in March 1909. The team played a total of 45 games, 17 of which were won and six drawn. In a severe British winter with admission prices doubled to watch the tourists, the attendances did not cover the players' promised £1 per man per week expenses. Even with a reduction in those expenses by 10 shillings per week, the tour ended with a loss of, then, a huge amount of almost £450.

Mr Giltinan was declared bankrupt. Rosenfeld and a tough forward, Patrick [Paddy] Walsh signed for Huddersfield and on 12 March 1909, 29 tourists, including Albert Rosenfeld, returned to Australia on the SS Suevic. In a magnanimous gesture, the Northern Union paid the return fare for the members of the tour and provided some pocket money for all the returning tourists. Several players stayed behind to end the season for their new British clubs, second rower Paddy Walsh [Fartown], North Sydney's Andy Morton, centre Jim Devereux [Hull], centre Sid Deane and scrum half George Anlezark [Oldham]. Others who would return for the following season were Rosenfeld [Huddersfield], Tom McCabe [Oldham], full back Mick Bolewski [Leigh], Dan Frawley and Lawrence O'Mally [Warrington]. The Wire also brought over Stuntz, an Australian player, and several good New Zealanders joined British clubs, full back H.S. Turtill [St Helens], H. Rowe an All Black wingman [Leeds] and the strapping forward, W. Trevarthen [Huddersfield]. This really was the vanguard of players who paved the way for mostly good, honest Kiwis and Aussies who came here to make money but also gave great service to the clubs and, more importantly, to the game. They brought colour and excitement to the dull, cold winter afternoons. The genius of Albert Rosenfeld helped immensely as did his New Zealand centre partner, the strong running former All Black Edgar Wrigley, who also toured with Baskerville's team. Another Australian took Wrigley's place when Tommy Gleeson went to Fartown and the superb three quarter line of Moorhouse, Wagstaff, Gleeson and Rosenfeld, the corner stone of 'The Team of All Talents', was born. Rosenfeld was a sturdy 12 stones at his best, around 5 feet 6 inches tall. He had a quick burst of speed, timed at 10.5 seconds for 100 yards, electrically fast in those days, this time would still be considered speedy today.

Lots of other good Australian players arrived in Britain and the Leeds club were always in the hunt for Aussies or Kiwis. A great centre, Aussie J. 'Dinny' Campbell arrived from Penrith, cost Leeds £350 on signing and £2 per match in 1912. He stayed with the club for eight years. When 'Dinny' went home he acted as the Leeds representative in Australia and recommended many great players to the club. New Zealander Charlie Seeling starred for Wigan as a forward and in 1910 the historic first Lions Northern Union tour of

Australia and New Zealand, with Jimmy Lomas [Salford] as captain, took place. The Lions touring team's colours then were red and white hoops and blue shorts. The following tour of 1914 saw a wingman of exciting calibre play against the Lions, Harold Horder [South Sydney and North Sydney].

In May 1908, Hunslet beat Oldham by 12–2 at Wakefield Trinity's ground to win the Championship after a replay, the first game ending at 7 points all at Salford. This gave the Parkside club a marvellous first when they won all the four cups available to them in one season. It was only emulated twice more in the game's history by Huddersfield and Swinton. The four cups Hunslet won were the Yorkshire Cup, the Yorkshire League, the Challenge Cup, won in a blizzard at Fartown, Huddersfield by 14–0 and the afore-mentioned Championship. This was a stupendous achievement with not an overseas player in sight.

The Leeds club, so active over the years in securing overseas players, signed their first ever overseas player on a short contract. The player was J.A. Lavery, a New Zealand wing three quarter from Christchurch, who had toured with Baskerville's team and whose 10-game career for the club produced four tries. Joseph Lavery then moved across the Pennines to play for the Leigh club. Several of the first Australian tourists either stayed on to play Northern Union Football after the tour or returned to play for various teams after firstly going home. One of the greatest of them was Albert Aaron Rosenfeld, who along with a much later fellow Aussie, Brian Bevan, was one of the most prolific try scorers in the game's history. Into the 1920s Leeds led the way with great overseas signings. Frank O'Rourke, the Sydney University and New South Wales centre was secured and shortly after the man described as 'the best stand off half in Australia', Jeff Moores, the Queenslander, arrived to create a very special partnership with O'Rourke. Wigan signed a trio of Kiwi 1926 tourists, Len Mason in the pack, centre Ben Davidson and speedy wingman, Lou Brown. Not to be out done, St Helens brought over wingman Roy Hardgrave and tough forwards Len Hutt and Trevor Hall, all three players were New Zealand internationals.

Jeff Moores the Leeds Aussie went home for a holiday and came back with an outstanding wingman whose deeds are still spoken of at Headingley, Eric Harris, the 'Toowoomba Ghost'. He was named after the Challenge Cup final of 1932 at Wigan's Central Park, when Harris zoomed past Scott, the Swinton full back, on the touchline to score the winning try and bring the cup to Leeds. Scott was asked how Harris had managed to beat the normally superb tackling full back, 'I went in to tackle him as I have done hundreds of times before, lined him up and went in low but he had vanished, like a ghost', replied Scott, hence the nickname. Harris had not vanished; he had simply displayed his remarkable change of pace by seemingly running flat out but suddenly hitting another gear and accelerating away.

At about the same time that Harris arrived, Leeds also introduced 1929 Kangaroo tourist half back Joe 'Chimpy' Busch from Sydney's Eastern Suburbs. Also from that tour, Bill Shankland, a full back with Eastern Suburbs joined Warrington and Cecil Fifield of Western Suburbs came to Hull FC. Another 'Roosters' star, the prolific scorer, Dave Brown, came to Warrington. A clash of clubs occurred when Wigan signed Hector Gee the scrum half and Joe Wilson the wing three quarter, both from the Ipswich club in Queensland and both international players. The clash happened because there was an agreement between Australia and Britain that no Australian player would be 'poached' whilst the tour was ongoing. Leeds again showed outstanding initiative by signing the huge success of the 1933 Aussie tour, the great stand off Victor Hey of Western Suburbs. Like Eric Harris, Vic Hey went on to become a legend for three clubs, Leeds, Hunslet and Dewsbury.

In 1937 the tremendous signing by the newly formed London club, Streatham and Mitcham of the famous Maori All Black full back, George Nepia caused a stir. Nepia moved up to Halifax, at Thrum Hall, and played for a short time alongside another former All Black, Charlie Smith, the big, strong running Maori. In 1947 an agreed five years' ban to stop any movement of players from one country to the other was put in place. The players who just beat the deadline of the ban were amongst the finest footballers ever seen in this country and to my mind we entered the best period in the game's history for classy entertainment.

Australians, Kiwis, South Africans and South Sea Islanders graced the game for many years. A legendary player from Blackball, a mining town on the West coast of the South Island of New Zealand, Ces Mountford, joined Wigan and became arguably the best stand off of his era. His fellow countryman, Brian Nordgren, a strong, fast wingman was also at Wigan and the pair brought much excitement to the already superb Wigan side of that time. Leeds signed that grand full back and goal kicker H.E. 'Bert' Cook, a war time New Zealand rugby union international. A wonderful Kiwi centre, Tommy Lynch, came to Halifax and Bradford Northern invested heavily in Kiwi talent by signing the great All Black wingman Jack McLean. They did this just after four cracking rugby players, full back Joe Phillips, centre Bill Hawes, wingman Norman Hastings and half back Bill Dickinson arrived. A 'flying' sprinter, Peter Henderson, who was also an All Black, came to Huddersfield and enthralled the Fartown faithful with his outstanding pace. Still the Australian players continued to pour into the country, just beating the five years' ban. The brilliant footballer and extremely tough Aussie, Arthur Clues, without doubt the best forward that I ever saw, came to Leeds and made his debut against Hull FC at Headingley on 1 February 1947. Unfortunately Clues didn't play again for eight weeks because of 'the second ice age' taking hold and covering the whole country with deep snow and thick ice.

Big Arthur took on the whole British pack in the 1946–47 tour series and his continued vendetta against the likes of Ken Gee, Joe Egan, Doug Phillips, Frank Whitcombe and George Curran was a feature of play for seasons after his arrival. Ted Verrenkamp was another good Leeds import as the Aussies continued to roll into Headingley. The Australian imports included Queenslander 'Wallaby' Bob McMaster, the professional wrestling prop and former rugby union international, his mate from the union days, Ken Kearney, the hooker who came back on two tours, one as captain. Keith McLellan another Aussie union convert and school master from Wollongong skippered Leeds in the centre in the Wembley win over Barrow in 1957. Bruce Ryan, the nightclub crooner and exciting running wingman, from Hull FC came via the Newtown club in Sydney. Len Kenny the side stepping wingman and Bob Bartlett the classy centre who was initially signed by the Bramley club, playing behind and stripping in the Barley Mow pub on Bramley Town Street, all graced the blue and amber of the famous Leeds club.

Another great Queensland forward joined Barrow then quickly transferred to Warrington, Harry Bath, who together with Arthur Clues formed the historic second row partnership for New South Wales in Australia and for the Other Nationalities in this country. The Great Bev, Brian Bevan, the spindly legged, bald, slender Aussie who looked too old and thin to play with those big bruisers yet was untouchable as a try scoring wingman, was another to cherish his primrose and blue Warrington jersey. Workington Town had some good Aussies, classical centre Tony Paskins, John Rupert Mudge (a tough forward), rugged front rower Bevan Wilson and utility back, 'Fizzer' Dawson. Trevor Allen the former Wallaby international captain and centre came to Leigh and was a brilliant capture. He was a distinctive player wearing his head guard or scrum cap in the backs as this was something we had not seen in this country since Dave Brown at Warrington, well before the Second

World War. Rex Mossop had a spell at Leigh too and his rugged play in the second row earned him an Aussie Test jumper.

Jeff Burke was another tough Aussie forward who gave good service to Leigh. Then there was the brilliant trio of Australians at Huddersfield. Lionel Cooper the big, ebullient wingman and high try scoring Test player was one part of the trio. The second part of the trio was Pat Devery, the silky smooth Test centre or stand off, whose magic skills mesmerised opponents and created many openings for Big Lionel and Peter Henderson. The last player of the three was the most exciting runner and fearless tackler ever at full back, the peerless Johnny Hunter. Cooper and Hunter came from Eastern Suburbs and Devery from Balmain, three of the finest ever to come over.

Wigan were one of the first to sign South African players when Van Heerden, a free scoring wingman and Van Rooyen, a big, tough forward joined them. In the immediate post war years, Leeds brought over a huge second row forward, Jack Pansegrouw. Pansegrouw later joined Halifax, playing at Wembley in 1949 when the great Bradford Northern side beat the 'Fax 12–0.

Not all South African imports made the grade. Wakefield brought over one of the top Springbok back row forwards, 'Iron Man' Ivor Dorrington who held 43 caps for South Africa but he found the pace of the pack in rugby league far too fast for him and he lasted only 12 games. When asked why he thought he had not hit the top at this new game he replied with honesty, 'I'm too old and too cold'. A second player from the same area, Jan Lotriet, a 6 foot 3 inch centre arrived at Belle Vue but failed to gain a regular place. The successful Springboks were excellent players, notably Alan Skene the regular Western Province centre who had represented South Africa in test rugby union. Skene's partnership with the great Neil Fox was one of the classic parings, the rapier and the broadsword.

Another South African, the international utility back Colin

Greenwood, came to play in England and was a huge success. Jan Prinsloo, another Springbok, was transferred to Wakefield from St Helens. Full back Fred Griffiths, a big kicker of a ball, was snapped up by Wigan from South Africa and St Helens signed the super wingman Len Killeen from the Southern Hemisphere country. Wilf Rosenberg, a dentist from Cape Town, arrived at Headingley and was an immediate favourite scoring 44 tries in the 1960–61 season before moving East to the city of Hull to carry on his great finishing at the Boulevard. The lightening quick Trevor Lake scorched the touchlines at Wigan as the Rhodesian flyer clocked up many tries at Central Park. The master signing from South Africa was that of Tom Van Vollenhoven. Van Vollenhoven (of St Helens) along with the other two greats, Brian Bevan (Warrington's Aussie) and Billy Boston (Wigan's barnstorming Welsh wingman from Cardiff) were the best three wingmen since the Second World War.

A few Fijian players made the grade here such as Jo Levula, Orisi Dwai, Laitia Ravouvou and an outstanding forward, Apisia Toga. A few Frenchmen spent some time playing rugby league—the best French player was French international Patrick Entat who led Paris St Germain in the initial Super League. One Italian player, Tony Rossi, joined Wigan then moved to Blackpool Borough.

The games in the European Championship resumed in 1945–46 and were played that season between England, Wales and France. In the 1949–50 season the Other Nationalities team were added. This team contained 'overseas' players and Europeans whose country did not enter a team, such as Scotland and Ireland. Quite a few Scots played rugby league, possibly the best known would be Davie Valentine of Huddersfield who captained the first World Cup winners, Great Britain in France 1954. The Other Nationalities teams were cracking sides, crammed with top Aussie and Kiwi players and played some brilliant stuff. The partnerships of Cooper and Paskins and Devery and Bevan were tremendous and the superb play of the two second rowers, Clues and Bath was outstanding. This side won the European Championship in 1952–53 and 1955–56. I suppose it would be difficult in today's climate to bring back the Other Nationalities because of contractual problems with clubs. But what a delight it would be to watch these masters at play and what a great workout it would be for the Great Britain squad before a Test series if they were to play either the Aussies or the Kiwis. The old game has had many admirers and many players who travelled thousands of miles to play it. Maybe it's a sign of age but somehow the overseas players who graced the game before Super League seemed to offer more than today's imports.

4

TRAVEL—BEFORE MOTORWAYS—AND TRAINING

The motorways were a godsend. The M62 traversing the Pennines was not only a masterpiece of civil engineering, it was the opening up of the country, almost like the wagon trains opened up the Wild West. Taking Leeds as the centre point, to the East, Hull suddenly became accessible for the games at the Boulevard to take on Hull FC. A touch farther across the city it was no more than an hour to Craven Park to play Hull Kingston Rovers. To the West travelling to the usually awkward venues of Leigh, Wigan and St Helens became like a stroll in the park. Rochdale, Oldham, Salford and Swinton became a 30 to 45 minute drive whilst St Helens was the furthest as a link onto the East Lancs Road that brought Leigh as the first turn off and Saints a wee bit further along the same decent stretch of road. Travelling from the West Riding Wigan was best approached via the M62, onto the M61, off at the Horwich [Reebok] exit and down to Central Park through Aspull. On the club coach, the journey took around an hour as opposed to a minimum time of two and a half hours on the old roads.

Going the old way the team bus would head through Huddersfield, Marsden, pass the Floating Light pub, skirt around Oldham, head for Prestwich, bear left towards Tyldesley, on to Hindley, through Ince and on to get your backside kicked at Wigan.

To Rochdale one took a slightly different route and passed the pub which had as its landlord the great Gus Risman. The pub was Nont Sarah's and it was bleak and awkward when travelling to Widnes and Warrington. Always out to the A580, the East Lancs Road, then turn off left and drive for an age through a landscape that seemed uninhabited. Leigh was off to the right on the East Lancs at the hotel on the cross roads. Carry on to Saints then a left off the main drag and an almost immediate right up to the ground. York away wasn't too bad from the West Riding and the trip outward to play the game was always the glum trip. Coming home was usually the fun time with some of the players entertaining the rest.

I remember a trip to York with the 'A' team when coaching at good old Bramley. I was the first team coach and always went with the assistant coach to check how the kids were doing. The secretary was always trying to cut corners with finances and when we arrived at the old McLaren Field ground, there waiting to take the lads to Clarence Street was a green double-decker bus, complete with a handle on the outside, above where the driver sat, and one turned it to describe destination of the bus. Well, you may guess, the youngsters were all over the bus, turning the handle to find 'York'. One or two smoked in those days and the non-smokers made the smokers go upstairs! There were several bells both up and down stairs and they rang every other second. One player asked if he could nip over and buy some sweets for the trip from the general store across the ground. He was back in no time carrying a brown paper bag. The bus set off and had hardly gone to the end of Town Street when we heard the ringing of a conductor's clipping machine. On turning around, there was the lad who had gone to the shop, resplendent in a child's conductor's outfit, calling out in a voice like the TV programme, *On the Buses*, 'Fares please...pass down the bus please...have your money ready please...tickets please'. The 'conductor' shifted a couple of lads upstairs who were smoking, threatening to bring the driver to them if they gave him cheek and it was hilarious. It was a fun trip out and we beat York 'A' easily that afternoon.

The trips East to Humberside had an obligatory stop at Boothferry Bridge and usually a cup of tea was waiting, followed by a walk to stretch one's legs whilst the directors had a cup of something stronger than tea. Players had to take that walk in hail, snow, wind, rain or during an earthquake. After about a mile the bus would approach the players slowly, everyone jumped on and away they went. You always came home in the dark in those days and went straight home if you had lost. There was no stopping under any circumstances and there were no toilets on the bus, only a battered old bucket wedged upright near the back seats. That bucket was for every use and I am not joking.

A true story about a bus bucket occurred on a rainy day on one of the long hauls to Barrow. I had signed an Australian, on match terms only, who had shown up at Bramley asking for a game. In those days you simply asked the player if he was clear to play with no strings from his home club and no bans from any other league or club. If the player said he was clear then you could register and play him immediately. This kid looked the part and had trained well. He told us that his last job at home in the north of Queensland had been as a cane cutter, rough work in the sugar cane fields. The board at Bramley were all elderly gentlemen of the old school consisting of a bank manager, a retired headmaster, a top postmaster and a couple of business men. All were strict, clean living men and when they were present, one behaved one's self. We were on a stretch of road, miles from civilisation when the Aussie called to me, 'Morrie, ask the driver to stop mate, I need the toilet real bad!' To ask the driver to stop would have meant that I would be shot immediately and I asked the Aussie if he could wait a while longer, 'Mate, I've only got this one pair of strides and I aint spoilin' 'em', and with that he pulled the bucket into the middle aisle of the bus and squatted. All the bus windows were shut because of the cold, wet weather and the heater was at the back of the bus going full belt. Gradually the aroma drifted down the bus to where the board sat. One by one the entire board of directors turned around to witness the Aussie sitting on the bucket! They quickly produced handkerchiefs and held them tightly to their noses.

The chairman stood up waving his arms, like Moses parting the Red Sea and called out, 'Driver, stop the bus!'

The club secretary, a real nice gentleman, supported his chairman by demanding, 'Young man, remove yourself from this saloon'.

The Aussie stood up, pulled up his 'strides', said to me, 'Sorry mate I couldn't wait'. He picked up his shoulder bag retired from the saloon and was never seen again. We were miles from anywhere. How he managed to find his way from the back of beyond I will never know.

A footnote to this story was that after about a mile further on, our cheeky little scrum half called down the bus, 'Chairman, who's going to empty this bucket?' The silence was deafening.

The trips up to Cumberland were not always so exciting. I have travelled up to the far north on a team buses on many occasions. They were horrendous journeys which had nothing to do with a bucket. Travelling on lane roads for mile after mile took hours and the return journey in the dark meant you would be lucky to get home by midnight. I have also travelled up to Cumberland on the train, always from Leeds to Carlisle then onto a waiting bus and across to Whitehaven or Workington. We always went up and down in the day, no staying overnight. Barrow was a long bus trip with no train. The trips to Castleford and Featherstone seemed like heaven, until you arrived and kicked off then you wished you were on the bus to Cumberland! The local trips to Bradford, Hunslet or Keighley would be by service bus, the term used was 'make your own way' just to save a few bob. Then the poor coach would be scratching around if a couple of players were late.

I took part in the game for a long time as a player and then as a coach and I witnessed many changes in travel. Radios, TVs, toilets, air conditioning, lovely soft seats that reclined, wow, what a change. Hardly anyone had a car when I signed for Hull in 1953. Roy Francis, our coach allowed the Leeds-based kids to have Thursday off but we had to train at our local amateur club. I trained at Buslingthorpe Vale and had to get one of the committee to sign a card saying I had trained. I found out later that someone from the Boulevard phoned up every Friday to check on my training and how hard I had trained. Every Tuesday in the season we, the out of towners, had to train at Hull. My training schedule each Tuesday began by taking a half day off work, without pay, boarding the 12.45pm train at Leeds station and travelling to the Paragon Station in Hull arriving at 4.45pm. Then I'd take a trolley bus along Anlaby road to the Boulevard or take a quick walk through the streets to the Medley Street Baths for a hard slog under coach Francis from 5.45pm to 7.15pm. Then I'd rush back to the Paragon Station to board the 8.00pm train to Leeds to be back in Leeds for 11.10pm. I'd catch the last bus up Cardigan Road and walk into my mam's at 11.20pm on the dot. If I missed the 8.00pm train in Hull, the next one arrived in Leeds at 5.30am the following morning.

I had to do that every Tuesday. Later when I was coaching, some of the players could see the ground from their home and would still be late. I used to go up the wall with them. I can tell you that the same kid was never late twice. If the ground at Buslingthorpe Vale was waterlogged as it sometimes was, I had to let them know at the Boulevard. Having phoned from a call box near home, I would go running around Woodhouse Moor, not too far from home. The Moor was three miles in circumference and surrounded by a tarmac path. I would run at various speeds, exercise vigorously at three designated points and continue running for about two hours then return home. When my parents went to bed, I would fill the old tin bath in front of the fire and have a good soak. I had an old skipping rope and on occasion went into the toilet area three doors down from home and skipped for ages in a big flagged area at the side of the toilets. Someone once told me that skipping was good for speed, stamina and a great help for your heart. I used skipping and boxing sessions for my teams when I went into coaching as in those days a coach had to be the conditioner too!

At Bramley when the weather was bad we would run onto Bramley Fall Woods and train on the grass under the big yellow street lights. Only as I matured into an experienced coach did the use of weights dawn on the majority of club coaches, although Vince Karalius, the great forward of St Helens and Widnes had seen the benefit that weights could give you early in his playing career. Vince was a nationally-known great trainer himself and folk lore within the game tells of Vince, after a tough training session at Saints, regularly running home to Widnes from Knowsley Road, St Helens. The training times were always Tuesdays and Thursdays and had been since the Ice Age. The training methods were a little more modern, they were from the Stone Age.

All the coaches I played under in those good (and bad) old days used the same psychology, which was to bore players to death with exactly the same training every Tuesday evening. Run, exercise, run, exercise, lap after lap, even the exercises were the same, press ups, then sit ups, then star jumps. The dramatic change would be that after 10 press ups on the first lap players would do 20 on the second lap. Football? You never saw a football on Tuesday evenings, apart from a game of touch and pass at the end of a session for about 20 seconds before the coach called out, every time, 'Don't be late on Thursday and don't forget, it's a tough 'un this weekend'. Even if the team had a week off the coach would say the same. A delightful change occurred when the ground was waterlogged, as often happened in the depths of winter, because the evening's work would consist of running up and down the grandstand terracing. You would start by running up and down in straight lines, then up and down, the full length of the stand, in diagonal lines. Another favourite coach's ploy was for players to carry a team mate, piggy-back fashion, up and down the terrace steps. Thrilling! It was worse for the poor lad on your back as he was jogged around wickedly. Tackling? We never did it in case someone got hurt but you were expected to know how to tackle. Defensive game plan? Just stand opposite a man and knock him over if he received the ball, sometimes if he had no ball!

One coach I played for was a bit of a forward thinker and used to advise us to use the 'mad dog and paling fence' style of defensive ploy. One had to stand one's ground in an unwavering line across the field and imagine the ball carrier opposite as a mad dog. You were a paling in the fence and if you went missing the mad dog would run through the gap you had left and bite you. We tried an umbrella style under another coach which employed the two end men of a line of about seven men dashing forward with the remainder creating an inverted 'U' which was designed to envelope the ball carrier and stop any short support work by the opposition. The sliding defence and its varieties were a thing of the future. Key players of the opposition were 'targeted' as they say today. Some coaches then didn't beat about the bush, 'Get to so and so and give him a clout. He doesn't like it'. To be honest I never knew anyone who did like taking a clout! The more sophisticated amongst the coaches would whisper to you, 'Don't forget, introduce yourself early to so and so'. Another regular piece of advice was, 'If a fight starts, one in, all in', and this was because the philosophy was that, 'He [the referee] won't send everyone off'.

On the training field the thought of using the free standing tackle bags, or a scrimmaging machine was tantamount to blasphemy only because:

1] the club couldn't afford them, and
2] those puffs playing rugby union use them.

The more humane coaches used things like shuttle running or the type of fitness and stamina running called 'fartlek', in which one ran over varying and undulating rises and dips. The running was done at various speeds or even walking over some distances. This was interesting but way too radical for the hard line, old fashioned thinking of most coaches.

When players finally retired from playing the game, some took to coaching because they had played for years and were involved with team mates. It was usually a mistake for an ex-player to coach the team they played for. The old adage that familiarity breeds contempt is so true in this scenario. The old fashioned methods of this almost brutal type of training were, in most cases, rebuked by the training squad. Only weeks before the coach had been put through the same mill, with the same sweat and effort the squad were going through and now he stood there giving the orders. He was no longer 'one of them'. The squad would naturally expect their old mate to be 'easy' on them and a tough approach to training usually caused friction.

The most important change to training techniques came from the National Rugby League Coaching Scheme. The scheme operated for years but suddenly, under the guidance of National coaches Laurie Gant and Albert Fearnley, the scheme took off. Supported by all the committees at RLHQ, the scheme also found a new interest from the stars of the game. Big-name players began attending the scheme's courses and some clubs stipulated in players' contracts that they must attend courses and gain a coaching certificate. This meant the younger players had advice on skills, food intake and nutrition. The RFL later handed the coaching scheme to the British Amateur Rugby League Association (BARLA) who appointed Phil Larder as BARLA's senior coach. Phil worked closely with both the amateurs and the RFL as joint national coach. In this respect, Phil Larder totally modernised the scheme, bringing it into line with the similar Australian scheme. As the assistant senior coach at the time I was also the Great Britain professional coach. In my visits to rugby league playing nations, I noted all the various skills drills used by different countries and we incorporated them into a new and exciting coaching technique which was accepted throughout the league. The various drills included the use of the old free standing tackle bags, totally taboo before, and a new innovation, tackle shields. This apparatus was imported into Australia from the USA Grid Iron coaching manual then over to the UK via the crushing 1982 Australian 'Invincible' tour, in which the Aussies showed us just how much in front they had raced. Tractor tyre inner tubes were also used in drills to attempt to strengthen tackling. Despite the time and money the coaching scheme spent educating club coaches in the new way of conditioning and defensive drills some clubs still bought the new equipment, stacked it in a cupboard and forgot about it.

In my first spell as the Leeds club coach I was amazed, on my first training night, to find that when all the shields and bags were wheeled out they looked brand new and worse still, the ultra talented Leeds squad had no idea how to use them correctly. So behind were they in aptitude that the players laid the shields out like beds and several of the players stretched out on the shields resting! I soon put a stop to that and the squad quickly learned all the drills I had amassed in my trips abroad. Our defence improved out of all proportion and we went unbeaten in my first 18 games at the club. About this time I realised that the two nights' practice sessions, totalling around four hours, were devoted to physical training, with little time left for the vital practice of tactics and skills. I laid down the policy that fitness of players was not my responsibility, it was theirs, the players. I issued the notice to 'come to me fit' and the four hours practice could be devoted to the mentioned skills and game tactics. I worked out a 15 minute schedule of exercises that they could do at home three times a week plus a one hour run, half an hour out, half an hour in, once a week. The players liked this new training regime and the team's results improved immensely. At Headingley I had punch bags installed and boxing training took place on training nights, this not only gave added impetus of something new but also helped to sharpen up the team's upper body and arm strength and added to their stamina.

All this change of training was well before Super League and its full time conditioners. When offered my first professional 'A' team coaching appointment way back in 1971 at Dewsbury. I checked out what was going on in most sports at coaching level. I saw the great Don Revie had started something new by having his Leeds United team warm up out on the field before the game, so I thought if it was good enough for Leeds United, it was good enough for Dewsbury 'A'. I am sure that I was the first rugby league coach to take his team out on the field for the pre-match warm up. I remember the lads being shy and embarrassed but they soon became used to it and again this new innovation paid dividends. I used this method at every club I worked. At Leeds we used to warm up on the cricket field before games to the delight of the hundreds who stood watching before taking their places on the terracing.

There was a huge difference in the physical training of players from me signing at Hull FC as a 17 year old in 1953 to when I became a fairly experienced coach in the late 1970s. One story explains it well. When signing for Hull FC in November 1953, the great Roy Francis, without doubt the most forward thinking coach in that era stood beside me as I signed. He shook my hand and congratulated me on signing, then said something I have never forgotten, 'Now you are a Hull player there are three things that you must not do in training. Never swim, ride a bicycle or do any weight lifting because you will damage muscles that you need for rugby', and that is the truth. Today all these types of training are used as a fitness vehicle to play in Super League and all three are part of the blue print to aid fitness.

One wonders what yesterday's stars would have made of this modern training that the players of today are programmed to do. It is impossible to compare today's players with ones from a bygone age. But I wonder if a pair of wingmen such as Billy Boston and Mick Sullivan would have the same impact now that they did in their heyday? Would Arthur Clues, Harry Bath and Dave Valentine have the same effect they had in their great days? Would the great Bevan and Cooper have thrilled the crowds as they did? How many more goals would Jim Sullivan or Jimmy Ledgard have kicked had they had lighter balls and a stand up kicking tee?

Sprint work helped the players as most clubs had a cinder track somewhere in or near the ground. Spiked running shoes were a must in any good wingman's training gear as they used to say, 'They make you run on your toes and not on flat feet'. Ball work was done mainly on Thursday nights. Moves were worked, plans were made to beat such and such a team. Little ploys between the half backs and the loose forward were tried and tested. 'Scissors' movements between centres and their wing partners were perfected. Forwards practised their complicated moves from the play the ball and if a prop liked his own move, usually near the line, woe betide anyone who encroached in his area or line of run. We had a move at Dewsbury on my second spell as senior coach which was spectacular to say the least and involved three passes. This was a 'run around' pass and a switch back before a big second rower charged onto the final pass. The first three times we used the move, our forward ran 40 yards to score. We pinched the move from the Australian Rugby Union international side we'd watched playing on TV. It was a good move but if used 20 years before we would have all been given the sack.

Today's game seems to be devoid of moves. The only one used that resembles the old moves is the delayed miss pass put in behind a dummy runner. The whole onus on ball play today is to complete the six tackles allowed in the laws of the game, any move may cause a mistake and lose you the ball. I think this preoccupation with completing six tackles has made the game too predictable. Playing 'no mistake' football with the use of 'the first cab off the rank' tactics from each play the ball and the same type of kick time after time, always on the last tackle means we have lost the element of surprise, that unexpected thrill that excites the crowd. These days everyone knows what is coming next. The art of the stand off half is totally dead in the water. On a recent tour Australia actually came without a recognised stand off, so too the age old constructive play from the centre for his wingman. The ball handling forward, who possessed the ability to suck in several defenders and set up a brilliant play with a deft pass, is now virtually obsolete. The 'eternal' triangle, numbers 6, 7 and 13, whose crucial structured work involving vital aspects of team play has disappeared totally from the game. These inbred skills, so important to the British style of play, have been ripped out of the game and replaced by head down, bum up big athletes who are drilled not to pass the ball for fear of losing possession. Size, strength and fitness have replaced guile, alertness and skill in the professional game. The reality is that at all the clubs players are prepared like battery hens, each one the exact replica of every other hence the demise of the British successes in international Rugby League Football. The quicker someone has the nerve to revert to playing with the British style the quicker we will be able to restore the pride that was once our trademark.

5

DIRECTORS AND COMMITTEES

It was a great honour to be asked to become a member of the board of directors of a rugby league club and join the long list of hard working, experienced men who directed the paths of various clubs in the professional league. These men were fair, knowledgeable and experienced, well versed in the intricate workings of a very peculiar game. First it was of tremendous help if the directors were *au fait* with the many laws and bylaws within the game. They could only negotiate these tricky obstacles by having a good working experience of the game and a good deal of streetwise nous. The well organised clubs worked to a system at board room level considered vital to the success of a new board member. They would ask the new director to guarantee an amount of money—this amount varied from club to club. He, or later she, would be asked to serve at least one season with another experienced director, as an apprentice so to speak, on one of the many sub committees run by the general board. The teaching director would be in his final season in that capacity and the new director would take over in his second season. The task usually lasted only one or two seasons but it was the sole responsibility of the director once he was in situ. It may have been as 'A' team director, dealing with both first team and 'A' team coaches and being in total charge of the 'second team'. This would include attending all 'A' team matches, home and away, and reporting back to the general board on the form, attitudes and progression of the young players who were learning their trade in the 'second team' and looking to check the financial implications of running the 'A' team.

The new director's next task might well have been to act on the ground sub committee for a year. This involved looking after the upkeep and general maintenance of the ground, dealing with contractors, acquiring estimates for work, liaising with the police on match days, organising security for gate takings to the bank and all the match day security required. A year later and the still new director might well have been asked to serve on the club finance sub committee. This was a vital cog in the club's running as the incoming finances were the responsibility of this committee. To keep coming up with ideas about making money and implementing those ideas was a hard job. In the following few years, after serving on all the sub committees, the director would be honoured with the offer of being the deputy chairman or vice chairman of the club. In this capacity he would deputise for the chairman if he was indisposed and would have a say in all club matters. After a few more years the supreme accolade would be offered, that of becoming chairman of the club. The board would be confident that the new chairman had served a good apprenticeship in the dealings of the board's work. This was how it was done at the big clubs. At others it was not quite as well organised. I have worked as coach to clubs who would ask a stranger who had dropped the jackpot on the one arm bandit if he fancied the chairman's job.

The men who served on boards of directors in those days were not all wealthy men. Some clubs offered places on the board to a member of the supporters' club and by doing that gained the wholehearted support not only on the terraces on Saturday afternoons but in helping with finances and other club business. There was a great cross section of small business men, all genuine lovers of their club and the game, who stood guarantee for a sum of money, only payable in a case of financial urgency, and who worked without pay, putting in hours of dedicated service for the betterment of their club. These directors included plumbers, joiners, builders, grocers, small shop owners, caterers and even undertakers. There were also men of wealthier means such as doctors, accountants, civil engineers, national house builders and lawyers.

There were clever men, honest men, not so honest men and, on rare occasions, downright villains on the board. In rarer cases still, bloody idiots were on the board but the common denominator among all members was the love of their club. I worked with all kinds of men and can recall lots of conversations about football that I accepted with varying degrees of stupidity. One conversation in particular comes to mind from the time I was coaching the Dewsbury club in my first job as senior coach. This is perfectly true. We required an experienced stand off half urgently. My chairman told me that there was a little money to buy the man I suggested the then Halifax player and prolific scorer, Bruce Burton. One of the vice chairmen of the club spoke to me in all sincerity a short time later. 'Is it true that you intend to sign Bruce Burton?' he asked.

I replied that I would sign him if I could. This man, who had a big say in all club matters including me keeping my job or getting the sack, said, 'Well I don't rate him. All he can do is score tries and kick goals'. I rest my case!

Luckily not all members of boards were that stupid. At that time in the game a few clubs were still members clubs as opposed to clubs owned by a board of directors. The fundamental difference was that a members club was run by a committee elected into office by the members of that club who usually put up a few pounds as a bond. The club was still run on the wishes of all the members virtually all of whom were supporters. The committee run clubs were usually full of political undertones. Every committee member had eyes on the chair, some delusions of grandeur, but most just bided their time and waited.

Some, though, could not wait and one tale that has come down the years was of a small business man in the building trade who had served on the committee of a Yorkshire club for a season or two. Election time was at hand and the current chairman and all the club officers were to stand, hoping for another term. The business man too had to stand for re-election but he had bigger fish to fry, he wanted the chair to fulfil his egotistical needs. Now this man was one of nature's big hurdles, placed in life just to be awkward, with the personality of a rattlesnake. He had around 10 men working for him, all of whom supported the club but never before had the desire to enter into the back stabbing world of rugby league committees. The boss had come up with a novel idea. Knowing that the voting would be tight and that a couple of votes for or against could swing the ultimate prize of the chair, our business man issued a bull that every one of his male workforce would offer their financial bond, which he would pay, and put themselves up for election to the committee. This done, as the election of officers was the first item on the agenda, they would then vote for him as chairman and these 10 extra votes should see him home and dry to lord it and pontificate for at least 12 months. His workers, however, misread the script and did not cast one vote for their boss for any office at all. He was removed from the committee and never applied again. He lived the irony of having to keep his men in work, otherwise to have been seen to have attempted a coup and failed would have reduced his local business dramatically.

A board of directors on the other hand ran their club as a pure business and leisure venture, whilst gaining the local kudos that being a director brought. They had the responsibility of speculating their own money on occasion but by using the club as a profit making business they could usually pay their way with the club's own finances. They also decided club policy rather than their supporters. Together they discussed and entered upon ventures that their experience in business suggested would be for the good of the club. The club was theirs and they wanted success both on and off the field. Sure, all clubs, even the bigger clubs like Leeds, Wigan and Bradford have hit hard financial times but it was the strength and acumen of their directors who negotiated their recovery. Some shrewd men have propped up clubs for years with their sense of the business world and straight dealing. Some are wheeler-dealers, always looking for an angle to push their club to the top. Others are the more solid type who just pay the bills and enjoy the game for what it is. A little like the attitudes of the professional as opposed to the amateur, but rugby league clubs in the Rugby Football League had to run on professional lines, some were not quite as ambitious as others.

The clubs not quite as ambitious as others had a 'homely' feeling, the ultra ambitious clubs felt quite palatial. Headingley with its wealthy tradition and superb facilities was always akin to entering a very roomy palace or country house. Bradford's Odsal Stadium was so big it reminded one of the Coliseum with the field being the arena. Wigan's Central Park screamed out with success. Its tradition of winning, aura of brilliant teams and style of play smacked one in the face upon entering. The huge notice board above the players' entrance, on the official ground car park, with the lists of successes written in gold leaf forced one to read it. The superb, wide open spaces of Station Road, the massive home of the Swinton club, devoured one with its grandeur.

I know that almost all the clubs in the league were hungry for success and some could not reach the dizzy heights of Wembley appearances and Championship wins but never the less were always hard to beat and never gave anyone an easy ride. The committees did their best with limited finances, always with an eye on the club's bank balance. I have worked at clubs where gas and electric were cut off because of non payment of bills and others where floodlights were classed as dangerous by the local council and could not be used for months. I have known some clubs who couldn't afford to turn the floodlights on and brought their kick offs earlier to play in daylight. Folklore exists about teams sending out schoolboys to collect jam and marmalade jars to take to the jam works and collect one half penny each to pay wages or make repairs to their beloved ground. This may seem unbelievable in these days of the Murdoch millions but rest assured it did happen. That of course was in the bad old days of the depression of the early 1900s.

A true story concerning the modern game revolves around a club secretary who had signed a very promising junior in the face of opposition from a couple of big clubs. The lad agreed to his signing on fee and the secretary asked him where he worked and what time he finished. It transpired that the lad could take a tram from outside his works directly to the ground for Tuesday and Thursday training and the cost was 3*d*. [3 pence in old money]. The secretary agreed to pay the 3*d*. each time he left work to come training. After about a month the secretary called the lad into his office. 'Where do you alight from the tram coming to training?' asked the secretary.

'Oh, at the tram stop at the top of the lane, there,' he said pointing to the road about 25 yards away.

'Right,' said the secretary, 'in future alight one stop away from that stop and walk the extra 100 yards to the ground. The extra exercise will do you good, oh and by the way, where you alight in future is a fare stage and it reduces your expenses from 3*d*. per trip to 2*d*. per trip.' When challenged about being skinny with the club's money the secretary said, 'Ah yes, possibly you think that but this player is a youngster. If he stays at the club for another 12 years, at 2*d*. per week saved, times the 48 times he comes training in a season, times 12 seasons, then that becomes a substantial amount'. That is how the old secretary and paymaster used to think. The tales about some of the clubs' directors are hilarious, some of their tricks are even funnier. In 1954 I was sent from Hull FC on a one month lone to a West Yorkshire club. The winning money was £5 and we duly beat York to register a good win. The following Thursday I was on my way to take the bus home after training with £5 winning money burning a hole in my pocket. I stopped under a gas lamp and opened the brown wage packet. You can imagine my surprise when inside the packet was not a £5 note but two tickets to a dinner dance at the local Town Hall, cost, £2-10s. each.

But for all the dance tickets from smaller clubs there was some genuinely good money to be earned at the bigger clubs and some of the most unlikely clubs paid great money. Keighley and York were renowned for paying top money. These two clubs were somehow out on a limb, seemingly miles off the beaten track, therefore they had to pay good money to entice good players to travel from the big cities in both Yorkshire and Lancashire. The club would put on a small bus each training night to pick up before and drop off after training.

For years every club tried everything they knew to cut down on expenses for training. Players stayed away from the club and even asked for transfers because of the refusal to pay expenses. It was a perk of the job. Some secretaries sought advice from the various Inland Revenue offices and were told that they could tax expenses. What! Tax expenses! That was tantamount to being taxed twice on the same bus trip or gallon of petrol we all cried. Some players then took advice and were told that expenses were tax free! During a bus strike in Halifax, the players were told by the then great secretary, Mr Bill Hughes, not to put in any expense forms until after the strike. The buses rolled again and the first player to go up for his expenses was asked by Mr Hughes, 'And what are you asking as expenses?'

The player hesitated for a split second, then blurted out, 'Ten shillings!'

Mr Hughes almost exploded, 'What! Ten shillings?'

The player caved in and in a sheepish voice quickly muttered, 'But I will settle for half a crown!'

I was fortunate to coach under some excellent chairmen. These included Mr Harry Jepson as football chairman at Headingley, Mr Doug Alton at Bramley and again at Bramley with Mr Jeff Wine, Mr Ronnie Dobson at Halifax when he was football director and Mr Bill Hughes as chairman. I was also lumbered with some unspeakable chairmen! Relationships between coaches and chairmen have changed radically from the old days in the 1920s and 1930s to the modern game. Back in the old days of the game, the extremely powerful chairman at the Leeds club, Sir Edwin Airy, said to the then coach, Bill Smith, 'Smith [as they did in those days] go down to Leeds station and meet this new man we have signed. He is called Hey and is on the 3.00pm train from London'. This 'Hey' was only the current Australian international, Vic Hey. The directors had signed him without the coach, Bill Smith, knowing and in those days he would have been at sea for over six weeks.

We come to the late 1980s when, as the Leeds coach, I strongly recommended the club should sign young forward Lee Crooks from Hull FC for a then record fee of £150,000. I was at the board meeting to put my case for signing him when the company chairman, the late Mr Norman Shuttleworth, suddenly saw my point. He phoned the late Hull FC boss, Mr Roy Wardby, agreed a price there and then and nonchalantly pulled out his cheque book to write a cheque for £50,000, placed it in the centre of the table and said, 'Right gentlemen, I will need two further cheques for the same amount each'. Without hesitation two cheques were placed there within seconds and with a smile he turned to Mr Bill Carter the football secretary and said, 'I think the club can afford the VAT bill, can't it?' Bill Carter signed a cheque for the VAT and sped off to Hull in his car to do the deal. Eight weeks later the club sent me over to Australia, club class, to attempt to secure Garry Schofield. I did this for another world record fee of £155,000. The same thing happened with the Leeds directors at a meeting when I returned from Australia, three further cheques totalling £150,000 were planted on the table with the club putting in £5,000 plus VAT. One could call Leeds RLFC a great club.

When I first went to coach Wigan in 1981–82 there was a large contingent on the board. Later it was dramatically reduced to four members consisting of Jack Hilton chairman, Tom Rathbone, Jack Robinson and the great innovator and political infighter, Maurice Lindsay. Under this less top-heavy directorship the club strode forward to record wins of the Challenge Cup and was without doubt the most successful board ever in the history of the game.

The most comical of all directors was without a doubt the one and only Geoff Fletcher who was chairman of Huyton. He also became chairman of Runcorn Highfield, then Prescot Panthers. Geoff was a tough forward in his playing days for some of the best teams in the league. As a director with Huyton, Geoff would switch with one of his fellow directors season on, season off as chairman. The following tale happened when he was football director at the club. Geoff sported a natty wig and was always in smart order when attending board meetings. He had signed a big, young forward from junior football in St Helens and given the lad £250 in his hand at the start of the season, promising the lad another £250 at Christmas. Yuletide had almost arrived and there was no sign of the 250 smackers. The big, tough lad was itching to get his hands on the dough. On this particular day Geoff was picking his way to the board room through the winter's mud. As he passed the dressing rooms, the big lad came out and stood face to face with big Geoff. The lad fronted Geoff and said in a loud voice, 'Right Fletch, where's my money? If you side track me again you will get this', and thrust a ham like fist in front of Geoff's face. Geoff was very handy indeed and thought to himself, 15 years ago I would murder this kid, so in for a penny, in for a pound and with that thought, Geoff stuck the nut on the lad. Had Geoff hit him 15 years ago, the lad would have crumpled but now he just shook his head and hit Geoff on the button. Down went the director in the mud! His newly cleaned black overcoat was the first casualty, covered in the slime. His wig flew off and his shirt and new tie ripped. Not only did he take a shellacking, he also felt his age and could hardly breathe. It dawned on him that he had made a terrible mistake in nutting the lad.

Then 10 of the players came out of the dressing rooms and pulled the lad off Geoff and hustled him away whilst Geoff picked up his wig, dusted it off and slapped it on his head like a flat cap. He went into the board meeting torn to shreds, beaten up and full of mud. The chairman, Geoff's mate, looked at him in disbelief and uttered, 'What the bloody hell have you been doing?'

Geoff breathlessly replied, 'I've just been negotiating a contract.'

What a picture it would have made! A respected director wrestling for keeps with one of his club's players. It was not always like that but the story indicates the differences between the directors back then compared to now.

Mr H.H. Waller, first chairman of the Northern Union, was the total opposite of Geoff Fletcher. Former player and secretary of the great Brighouse Rangers club, Mr Waller, one of two brothers who worked their business as cotton spinners from the West Vale area of the Brighouse and Halifax district was later honoured when, as the fledgling Northern Union's first President, he was presented with a silver casket in appreciation of his devoted work for the union in its first two years of existence. In his later life, Mr Waller took to politics in the Greetland District Council.

The rather sedate, gentlemanly figures of yesteryear, with their wing collars, bowler hats and a very different set of values than today, gradually evolved into the totally professional world of today's highly financially orientated game of Rugby League Football. Looking logically at today's game, it had to develop into a ready made game for TV. Everything about the game seems purpose made for TV. Rules have been tinkered with to make the game absolutely presentable and suitable for that little box, some I think, detrimental to the game I knew as a boy. Nevertheless, without these small changes we might well have had no rugby league at all. The chance to grab Murdoch's Millions had to be taken.

The full time employment of players, even if I thought that it came too soon, was a natural progression. The little north country game, so parochial in its conception, so jealous of its own purity of birth and its kindred to the harsh life of northerners, was thrust, apparently overnight, in a blaze of publicity into the national game it is today. The days of the hundreds of coal miners who yearned for Saturdays to come around to taste the freedom from the claustrophobic job forced upon them by playing the game has gone, so too have the mines themselves. But the spirits of those grand gentlemen, the directors and committees, will forever be remembered as the brave people who made the first efforts to present the Northern Union to a world so different to the one we live in today.

6

REFEREES

Of all the positions of importance in the game, the one with the worst stigma of conspiracy and cheating was, and still is, the referee. Even in the days when rugby league referees were the strongest and most respected officials in any sport, there was a huge void between the referee and the paying public. Supporters of the amateur game would become incensed by some of the referees' decisions and occasionally attack the official. In the early days of the Northern Union the great side, Brighouse Rangers, were involved in two games in which the referees were assaulted. One game was at the old Parkside ground, the home of the Hunslet club, when a spectator hit Mr Rayner, the referee, on the shoulder as the Hunslet players and committee escorted him to the cricket pavilion. Then as he was crossing the cricket field after changing his refereeing clothes, someone else hit him with an iron bar. Mr Rayner praised the efforts of the Hunslet players and officials in their attempts to guard him during the frightening experience. The second incident took place at Rochdale Hornets ground when the referee, Mr J. Slevin of Wigan, was roughly handled after the game in which he disallowed a try and goal to Hornets which would have won them the game. On his way to the dressing tent people brandishing sticks and umbrellas struck him several times. He escaped in a hansom cab, escorted by a police detective and a Rochdale player, to the train station at Heywood. The train station was situated some miles from the station at Rochdale where a large crowd waited to remonstrate with Mr Slevin expecting him to depart from there on his homeward journey.

The breakaway in 1895 was a real leap into the dark in more ways than one. Imagine the logistics of moving referees around alone, as well as recruiting good men to officiate. One of the early good referees was Mr J.H. Smith [Widnes], a strict disciplinarian and a man whose word was accepted as law. If seen today Mr Smith would have caused a snigger or two refereeing in his knee length frock coat and knickerbockers. In wet weather, he wore a bowler hat! Despite his attire he controlled a game well, so much so that he officiated in many top games. His Challenge Cup finals were Batley versus St Helens (10–3 to Batley) in 1897 at Headinley, Batley versus Bradford (7–0 to Batley) in 1898 at Headingley, Halifax versus Warrington (8–3 to Halifax) in 1904 at Salford and Hunslet versus Hull FC (14–0 to Hunslet) in 1908 at Huddersfield. He was also in charge of the first ever Test against Australia in this country on 12 December 1908. The game was played at the Park Royal ground in London and ended in a 22–22 draw.

A rarity appeared in the shape of a Cumberland referee when Mr J. Kidd [Millom] took control of the 1901 Challenge Cup final played again at Headingley between Batley, the winners by 6–0, and Warrington. There were several referees who became legends at around that time, possibly the most famous was the Reverend Frank Chambers of Huddersfield. The Reverend Chambers was a former Huddersfield player under the old RFU regime and his calling to the cloth ensured his insistence of fair play and no blaspheming. He too was a strict man on all aspects of the game and, after retiring from refereeing, took to writing a column for his long time friend and publisher of the old Rugby League Review, Mr Stanley Chadwick of Huddersfield. Mr Frank Renton [Hunslet] was around a long time with the whistle. He controlled the 1900 Challenge Cup final between winners Swinton against Salford with a 16–8 score at Fallowfield, Manchester. He also controlled the 1907 final between the victors Warrington against Oldham (the score was 17–3) at the Broughton Rangers ground and then, 14 years later, the 1921 final between winners Leigh versus Halifax (13–0) also played at Broughton.

Oldham produced a fine referee in the form of Mr Bill McCutcheon. He took control of the 1906 Challenge Cup final at Headingley in which Bradford beat Salford 5–0, then was awarded the second Test against Australia on 23 January 1909. The game was played at Newcastle when Britain won 15–5. A great honour was given to the McCutcheon family when the then new double decked stand at the Watersheddings ground, Oldham, was named after them. The referee for the third Test on that 1908–09 Tour was Mr E.H. 'Ted' Smirke [Wigan] when the British team won again by 6–5 at Villa Park, Birmingham, on 15 February 1909. Mr Smirke also handled the 1909 Challenge Cup Final between Wakefield Trinity and Hull FC, won by Trinity with a score of 17–0 at Headingley. Another good Wigan referee at that time was Mr Ben Ennion who refereed the 1912 Cup Final at Headingley between winners Dewsbury who played Oldham (the score was 8–5). St Helens also had a good referee at that time in Mr J.F. May who officiated in three Challenge Cup Finals, 1911 Broughton Rangers versus Wigan—Broughton won the game 4–0 at Salford, 1913 Huddersfield versus Warrington (Huddersfield won 9–5) at Headingley and in 1914 Hull FC defeated Wakefield Trinity 6–0 at Thrum Hall, Halifax.

Arguably the most successful referee of his age was Mr Bob Robinson of Bradford. He refereed the last Challenge Cup Final before the close-down for the duration of the 1914–18 Great War where Huddersfield beat St Helens 37–3 at the Watersheddings ground, Oldham. His Test record shows a remarkable longevity. His first international game was in the shock defeat of Great Britain by Australia with a score of 33–8 in the third Test of 1911–12. Then he controlled the second Test of the 1921 Australian Tour at The Boulevard, Hull where Britain lost 16–2. He also refereed the 1927 Challenge Cup Final at Central Park, Wigan, when Oldham beat Swinton 26–7. Then in 1929–30 he refereed all four Tests of the Britain versus Australia series. Australia won the first, 31–8, at Hull Kingston Rovers ground, lost the second at Headingley 9–3 and drew the third 0–0 at Swinton. It was in the dying stages of this draw that Bob Robinson showed his courage. With only a short time left in the game, Australia attacked with venom and from a 20 yard scrum, Joe 'Chimpy' Busch, the Aussie half back, shot away in a diagonal run for the corner. Swinton's loose forward, Fred Butters, raced after him all the way to the try line and as Busch dived over the line in an attempt to win the Ashes for his country, Butters arrived with the perfect leg tackle which swept Busch across the touch in goal line. The touch judge immediately raised his flag to signal the player had crossed the in goal line before touching the ball down. Mr Robinson bravely blew for touch despite continuous serious harassment from the tourists.

The fourth Test was played on Wednesday 15 January 1930 at Rochdale Hornets ground before a crowd of 16,751 people and again the score was 0–0 until a few minutes from time when wingman Stanley Smith went zooming over to score the winning try. Never had a Test series seen such tenacity and downright effort. The man in the middle of all that effort and determination to win was Bob Robinson, the Bradford referee. Also in 1929, Bob Robinson refereed the first ever Challenge Cup Final to be played at Wembley Stadium when Wigan beat Dewsbury 13–2. He was in control of the Leeds versus Halifax game at Headingley on 25 March 1932 when the grandstand burnt down causing the referee to abandon the game and save many lives by his quick action. Without doubt Bob Robinson was one of our best ever referees.

In 1924 the Reverend Frank Chambers had charge of the game that saw the then record crowd of 41,871. Because this Challenge Cup Final was an all Lancashire tie the game was taken to the Athletic Ground at Rochdale. At that time the Hornets' home ground was just about the biggest ground available but even then the crowd invaded the pitch only half an hour before the kick off. Mounted police had to force the crowd back into the terraces. The star wingman for Wigan was the free scoring former Springbok international Van Heerden, who along with fellow Springbok, tough second rower Van Rooyen, were the strong men in the Wigan set up. The touchlines had to be cleared several times as the Reverend Frank demanded a fair game be played and encroachment of spectators onto the field did not constitute a fair game. The mounted police were told to stay on the perimeter of the pitch so that the crowd could be kept from the playing area. With Oldham playing well, suddenly Van Heerden gained possession inside his own half and chipped over the heads of the Oldham defence, re-gathered, side stepped two Oldham tacklers, handed off a couple more and rounded a mounted policeman to trot around under the posts. The Reverend Frank awarded the try and the score enabled Wigan to tear ahead by 21–4 and lift the Cup.

The Great War ended the playing of wholly competitive rugby as the Northern Union had over 1,500 players in the armed forces. As the fierce fighting in the trenches began in earnest the lists of killed and wounded players mounted. The dead included three players just back from the Lions 1914 Tour of Australia and New Zealand, Bill Jarman the Leeds forward, Fred Longstaff the Huddersfield forward and Walter Roman the big Rochdale Hornets forward. Other players who lost their lives included George Thom [Salford], J.H. Turtill [St Helens], George Thomas the Warrington forward and John [Jack] Harrison, VC and MC of Hull FC. Harrison was an officer and flying wingman decorated twice for bravery in the field of battle.

During the 1920s and 1930s our referees continued to prove the best with Mr R. Jones [Widnes] carrying on a great tradition from that town by officiating in the Rochdale versus Hull Cup Final of 1922 at Headingley, Rochdale winning 10–9, and the Oldham versus Hull Kingston Rovers Cup Final of 1925 at Headingley which Oldham won 16–3. The West Riding also produced some first class referees, Mr A. Brown [Wakefield] taking the 1926 final won by Swinton 9–3 against Oldham at Rochdale. In 1928, Mr H. Horsfall [Batley] controlled the Swinton versus Warrington final at Wigan— Swinton won the match 5–3. This game was notable as it was the fourth consecutive season that the Oldham club reached the final, winning two and losing two. How sad that Oldham, such a force in the Challenge Cup in the middle 1920s, could not maintain that cup form for a little longer and reach the finals played at Wembley which started in 1929. They are one of the few clubs who have never played in the final in London. Mr F. Mills [Oldham] refereed the 1920 final at Headingley when Huddersfield beat Wigan 21–10 and the 1923 final at Wakefield where Leeds were victorious over Hull FC with a score of 28–3. Widnes versus St Helens was the 1930 final controlled by Mr F. Peel [Bradford] which Widnes won 10–3 at Wembley. The year 1931 saw Halifax beat York in a 22–8 victory with Mr J. Edden [Swinton] presiding over the match again at Wembley.

Then in 1932 the final was dramatically moved from Wembley to Wigan to accommodate the Leeds versus Swinton final which Leeds won 11–8. The Wembley authorities cancelled the rugby league final that year as the RFL had to bring the date of the final forward to 9 April to enable the tour of Australia and New Zealand to take place. This date was too near the annual FA Cup Final, so our final was taken to Central Park. The referee was the excellent Mr Frank Peel [Bradford]. The same referee, Frank Peel, took charge of the Salford versus Barrow game in the 1938 Wembley final. Salford won the game 7–4. Another Frank, this time the alert Mr Frank Fairhurst [Wigan] took the 1933 final where Huddersfield beat Warrington 21–17 and this was followed in 1934 by Widnes losing to Hunslet 11–5 with the referee being Mr A. Holbrook [Warrington].

The Manchester-based Broughton referee Mr A.E. Harding had control of the all Yorkshire final of 1935 where the result went Castleford's way when they played Huddersfield and won the game 11–8. The 1936 final saw the debut of the great character and excellent referee Mr Albert S. Dobson [Featherstone] into the big-time world of the Wembley final. This 1936 final had, like most, a controversial moment when in the eighth minute, Eric Harris broke away down the right hand touchline. On approaching the Warrington full back, Bill Shankland, he put in a superbly delivered crosskick. As the crowd followed the flight of the ball, one lone Leeds player was sprinting down the middle of the field, he was Iowerth Isaac the Welsh loose forward, who caught the Harris kick on the full to dash over for the first try of the game. The Warrington players appealed for offside but Mr Dobson called, 'Play on!' and the try stood. The Leeds players had practised the crosskick all week in their preparations for the match and it worked first time! The grand but unfashionable club Keighley fought its way to the 1937 final. Opposing them were the tough Widnes outfit with the famous Shannon and McCue half back combination. The referee, Mr Paul Cowell, was again from the Warrington area. As described, Frank Peel took the 1938 final as another great referee appeared in charge of the 1939 Wembley showpiece, Mr George S. Phillips [Widnes]. This final would be the last genuine Wembley final until after the Second World War.

The next final at Wembley was a fantastic, pulsating affair just right for all the thousands of recently 'demobbed' troops home after five years away. The game was Wakefield Trinity versus Wigan and the referee was Mr Alf Hill [Leeds]. Wakefield Trinity won the game 13–12. But the semi-final between Wakefield Trinity and Hunslet was the most controversial one in the history of the old Cup. With Trinity leading 7–3, and the seconds ticking away late in the game, Frank Watson the Hunslet stand off pushed through a neat kick, inside his own '25', for his speedy wingman O'Neill. The speedster collected the ball, shot away, beating three tacklers and swerving past Teall the Trinity full back, ran diagonally 100 yards to dive over in a favourable place for the conversion. Sheer ecstasy turned to painful disappointment as Mr George Phillips the referee signalled 'no try' and ordered a penalty kick to Wakefield for O'Neill being off side from Watson's kick. The touch judge who called the off side was Mr C. Ramsden, who, as the try was disallowed, was attacked by an irate Hunslet supporter who had jumped from the terrace to the pitch to remonstrate with Mr Ramsden. The supporter struck the touch judge and was immediately arrested and hustled away into the dressing rooms by the police. O'Neill was totally exhausted from his mammoth run, Mr Ramsden was stretchered away suffering from a broken jaw, to be replaced by Mr E. Hopkins, a referee who was a spectator at the game. The attacker received a severe jail sentence. Twelve months later an all-Yorkshire final featured the two sides from the West Riding in the exciting 1947 game where Bradford Northern beat Leeds 8–4 with Mr Paul Cowell again in charge.

Social change in the immediate post war era was rampant. Tough, old fashioned players, particularly the forwards, held so much in check by the discipline of the old brigade of referees, were suddenly confronted by officials who seemed 'human'. This new breed started quietly calling players by their Christian names, for instance, 'Good tackle Joe, make sure you go a little lower next time and be careful with that elbow', or 'Leave it alone now Sam, I'll give you the benefit of the doubt this time but watch out in future'. Some players liked this type of verbal interplay with the official, others did not! One thing was for sure, the players soon figured out the new breed of referees. A quietly spoken word of advice given by the top referees when the official saw a sly punch delivered would, on occasion, wait until the receiver of the punch had gained retribution with his own return punch, usually later in the game. Then in would come the sound advice, 'Now then, that's one apiece. Leave it out now and call it a draw. No more or you both walk'. The vendetta was usually over then until the next time they met!

The Challenge Cup final was given to the referee who had shown good consistency throughout the season. The following two finals were both refereed by the ultra consistent Mr George Phillips of Widnes and both featured Bradford Northern. In 1948 Bradford Northern lost to Wigan with a score of 8–3 but won against Halifax in 1949 with a score of 12–0. An unusual thing happened in the Championship Final in 1949. The final was played at Manchester City's Maine Road ground between Huddersfield and Warrington and the referee should have been the excellent Mr Frank Smith from Barrow. But Mr Smith was not informed of his appointment as his notification was lost in the post. A cruel stroke of luck occurred too as Mr Smith read that another referee had been appointed so he did not go to the game. It all had been an unfortunate mistake and on match day everyone was there except the referee. What had been atrocious luck on the part of Mr Smith turned out to be great news for Mr Matt Coates of Pudsey who should have been one of the touch judges in the big final. Matt Coates was catapulted into the limelight as controller of the game, refereed superbly and went on to greater things. Mr Paul Cowell of Warrington, the excellent referee, was at the game as a spectator and drafted in to run the touchline.

Mr Albert Dobson [Featherstone] took the 1950 'derby' final at

Wembley between Warrington and Widnes (won by Warrington 19–0) and in 1951 we saw the outstanding Mr Matt Coates [Pudsey] in charge of the Wigan versus Barrow game (Wigan won the game 10–0). The great Charlie Appleton of Warrington was the referee of the 1952 final when Gus Risman brought his hardy cup fighters down from Cumberland in the shape of Workington Town who took on those other wonderful Challenge Cup competitors, Featherstone Rovers. The legendary Freddy Miller was at full back for Featherstone and kicked two goals but it was not enough to stop Workington winning 18–10. Another Cup final beckoned for Mr George Phillips when he officiated in the epic 1953 game, remembered as 'Ramsdens Final' because of the outstanding performance by Peter Ramsden the Huddersfield stand off half. Ramsden was 19 years old that day and celebrated his birthday with a glorious match winning try. Saturday 24 April 1954 saw a drawn final at Wembley for the first time when an outstanding referee made his debut onto the big stage, Mr Ron Gelder [Wakefield]. Warrington and Halifax shared eight points with two goals from 'Tuss' Griffiths for Halifax and two from Harry Bath for Warrington. The replay was not until 5 May to allow Championship games to be played and the rematch was at the huge Odsal Stadium, Bradford, with an early evening kick off. Ron Gelder was the referee again and no one envisaged the massive turn out for this replay. The official gate was 102,575 and the crowd witnessed Warrington seal a memorable 8–4 victory.

Mr Gelder refereed the following two finals when in 1955 Barrow beat Workington Town by 21–12 and in 1956 St Helens beat Halifax by 13–2. Charlie Appleton controlled the 1957 Leeds versus Barrow final, Leeds lifting the Cup with a score of 9–7. The 1958 final was between Wigan and Workington Town with Wigan taking the Cup by 13–9, Ron Gelder officiating in his fourth final in five seasons. Hull FC and Wigan fought out the 1959 final with the experienced

Charlie Appleton in charge with Wigan triumphing by the biggest wining score of 30–13 since Huddersfield's 37–3 victory over St Helens in 1915. Ron Gelder also refereed the Great Britain versus Australia first Test of 1959 at Swinton which the Aussies won by 22–14 and the second Test at Headingley which the Brits won by 11–10. A change of referee for the third Test at Wigan saw Mr Eric Clay [Rothwell] take charge. His nickname of 'Sergeant Major' was seen to be true as he stood no nonsense whatsoever and Britain won by 18–12. Eric Clay was a big man who had seen service in the RAF. He was one of the referees who never missed a trick. He also refereed with common sense and was one of the foremost exponents of allowing players to settle arguments on the field so long as there were no blatant fouls. He was one of the old stagers who would say, 'One apiece lads, now cut it out', after a couple of blows had been thrown, or, after one player had 'got even' after taking one. Eric didn't mind allowing players to get even but he was always in charge of the game.

Another great referee who also demanded respect was Mr T.W. Watkinson of Manchester, as did his 'stablemate', Mr D.T.H. Davies, also of Manchester. Tom Watkinson had the cracking St Helens v Wigan 'derby' final on a baking hot 13 May 1961. Saints won the Cup by 12–6 and Mr Watkinson played his part well. The 1962 final was between Wakefield Trinity and Huddersfield with Dennis Davies in charge, Trinity winning the Challenge Cup by 12–6. Davis also had control in 1963 when Wakefield beat Wigan 25–10.

George Phillips and Ron Gelder dominated the period 1945 to 1960. At varying times, Matt Coates, Tom Watkinson and Dennis Davies along with Mr S. Adams [Hull], Mr A. Howgate [Dewsbury], Mr R.L. Thomas [Oldham] and the great Yorkshire character, Mr Laurie Thorpe [Wakefield] all took big league and cup games. Laurie Thorpe in particular was a referee with a wonderful sense of humour. He overcame a malformed spine to climb the refereeing ladder on merit. His on-field banter with the tough men of the day is legend amongst the elder statesmen who are still with us and who played under Laurie. Laurie is particularly remembered for his word for word battles with the great Arthur Clues. Clues' remarks about Laurie's disabilities would spark off a verbal but always good natured crossing of swords between the two men who were the best of friends after every game. Both Arthur and Laurie knew just how far they could go and players in the same game would be helpless with laughter at the pair's verbal antics. They kept their rapport low key, a word when Laurie was close up to the scrum, so only the forwards and big Arthur in particular could hear and the big Australian replied in the same vein. Laurie Thorpe was a great character and as befitting a great referee, Laurie died on the field of play whilst controlling a first team game at Whitehaven. He was sadly missed.

As I said earlier, a referee's lot is not a happy one, so goes the song. To the winning team's supporters, whoever the referee had been that day, he would be, 'The best we have had all season'. To the losers the same referee would be, 'The worst we have had. I don't know what the referees are coming from these days. Who picks 'em?' The referee just could not win. The cat calls to the referee were universal. After only a few moments calls of, 'Ger 'em onside ref', would ring around every ground at which a game was in progress. This was followed at every scrimmage in the game, from first to last, by 'Ger 'is feet back ref', or 'Yer blind bugger', or 'Loose arm ref'. Each time the ball was dropped, irrespective of whether or not the official had blown to halt the game, the whole crowd would call, 'Knock on ref,' each pass that endangered a side would be greeted by the defensive team's supporters with, 'Forward pass ref'. Other derogatory remarks that are never heard today were, 'Where did they dig yon fella one up from? He in't good enough to ref t'A team'.

There was no chanting and singing of foul mouthed songs as today but even in well attended matches these old insults would come through loud and clear. I think, on reflection, that the poor bloke whose job it was to implement some archaic law, say in scrimmaging, was on a hiding to nothing when one remembers the antics that both the hookers and props got up to in an effort to win every ball from every scrum. Referees had to be streetwise and know every trick in the book to stay alive with some of the experienced and villainous number nines who were around then. A huge problem within the game was the scrum. The laws at the time made it legal for the field side prop forward, or open side prop forward as he was known, to strike for the ball once it had passed his inside foot as he stood in the scrum. This led to many open side props selected only for their ability to win possession at the set scrum. A good open side prop would not allow the ball to reach his hooker as he won the ball. Some prop or hooker combinations would operate the blocking system where the hooker would not strike for the ball but block his opposing hooker's legs thus enabling his open side prop to win the ball virtually unopposed. The open side prop had a varied array of tricks for the differing type of scrum. If the scrum was awarded as his 'loose head', meaning his head was nearest the scrum half feeding the scrum, the prop would grip his opposite prop's shorts' leg and force it downwards, making it impossible for him to lift that leg and unbalance him. If the prop was 'against the head', meaning the opposing prop's head was nearest the half back feeding the scrum, he would come into the scrum at an acute angle, with his backside away from the scrum. This allowed him to wedge his head into the opposing hooker's face or neck and force his head upwards out of the scrum, simultaneously striking for the ball when it entered the scrum. It all seems very technical, considering the prop was supposed to be a person of little intelligence, but it was a skill and a test of strength. The scrum half too had a large input as to the legalities of scrimmaging.

Almost every half back had his own variety of tricks as to how to win the ball on his put in. Some would 'spin' the ball so that on touching the ground it would break towards his hooker. Another trick was to feed the ball onto the opposing hooker's shins so that the ball would ricochet back into his own forward's feet. Some would throw the ball hard, directly into the face of the opposing hooker. To use this ploy the half back had to come extremely close to the mouth of the tunnel of the scrum and if so, the wily open side prop could hook his outside foot behind the half back's backside and pull him into the tunnel, ball and all. When that happened the half back was fair game and received the kicking he deserved for attempting to disfigure the poor hooker.

Most referees would call a player over to him when he had committed a misdemeanour to tell the player, one to one, why he had been pulled out and what would happen if he did it again, all very close and personal. Not so Sergeant Major Eric Clay. He had his own way of doing things. The whistle would stop the game, a huge finger would point at the guilty party and an aggressive voice would bark out, 'Number so and so, here to me', and Mr Clay would then turn and walk about 10 yards away. The poor player had to walk, very coyly, after him until the big referee turned to deliver the mother and father of a dressing down and, with a wave of his hand, Mr Clay would despatch the player back to his team.

The period 1960 through to 1980 saw many top officials grace our game. The excellent, yet occasionally controversial, Mr Eric Lawrinson [Warrington], was one. It seemed that whenever Mr Lawrinson controlled a game something always happened that had the crowd talking! That was his style, he would keep the game flowing, sometimes ignoring the obvious knock on or forward pass which would drive the spectators crazy but Eric Lawrinson would, in the same game, seem to always produce a brilliant piece of refereeing that had the crowd cheering him. Mr Joe Manley, another real character and a fine official from Warrington, was a key referee in this period as was Mr Sam Shepherd from Oldham. Both controlled top matches.

Sometimes the very nature of our game produces a tragedy on the field. Many players have suffered terrible injury, some the worst possible scenario, death. When this happens to a crowd-pleasing, tough top international competitor in the prime of his career it is a sad occasion. On 1 May 1971, Mr Harry Hunt of Prestbury was controlling the Leeds versus Salford, second round Championship play off game at Headingley on a warm afternoon under a cloudless blue sky. Harry Hunt was a first class referee, who officiated in many important games. Mick Shoebottom, the Headingley darling and tough, stand up knock 'em down international utility back, went into the corner after one of his typical blitzing runs to register a try for Leeds. Challenged by the late, excellent Colin Dixon in the act of scoring, Mr Hunt awarded the try but Mick Shoebottom lay motionless just inside the flag. A sheer accident in that tackle caused Mick's premature retirement and his early death a few years later. The damage was a blood clot on his brain and anyone who witnessed the purely accidental incident will never forget the sight of the ultra brave Leeds back being carried off to the dressing room.

Other good men who made an impact in games they refereed in this period were Mr John McDonald [Wigan], Mr Alec Givvons [Oldham], the Headmaster from the York area Mr Gerry Kershaw [Easingwold], Mr Kevin Allat of Southport, Mr Peter Massey and Mr Vince Moss both from Manchester, Mr Ronnie Moore [Wakefield], the former professional player and poacher turned gamekeeper Robin Whitfield [Widnes], the effervescent and very likable Stan Wall [Leigh] and the equally likable international referee Mr Ronnie Campbell [Widnes]. Two of the most decorated referees in this period were the great Mr Billy Thompson [Huddersfield] and the superb Mr Fred Lindop [Wakefield]. Stan Wall served the St Helens club as a member of the back room staff and for many seasons carried out the kicking tee during matches for the Saints. When I was coaching and we had Stan as the referee I would impress on my players that Stan had the habit of giving the defending side a then 5 yard onside mark but just as the ball was being played, he would shuffle backwards about 18 inches and call out, 'Off side lads, get back to me'.

Stan was always approachable. I remember once walking off after a game at Thrum Hall, Halifax and after shaking hands with Stan saying to him, 'Stan, do you know that you take a step backwards at the play the ball and call off side even though you have given the team the mark?'

Stan smiled and said, 'Yes Maurice, I do know. Infuriating isn't it?'

From then on, no matter which team I was coaching, I would tell my players, 'Be careful today with Step Back Stanley'.

Another time Stan, who was a pit deputy during the Miners strike in the early-to-middle 1980s and still had to work during the strike, was asked by the colliery he worked at if he would take some NCB papers across to a colliery in Castleford. The miners accepted that workers could still do things like the paper work and allowed carriers of these papers in and out of the picket lines. As Stan approached the picket lines in his NCB van the miners suddenly shouted, 'Get that van!' and surged around Stan, rocking the van to and fro, 'Pull the bugger out!' they cried.

Stan held the papers up to the van window and called out, 'I'm on NCB business!'

But the huge miner nearest the window called back in, 'This has nothing to do with the strike. You are that blasted referee who cost Castleford the game last week with some lousy decisions. Get him lads!' Luckily the police rescued Stan just in time. Oh to be a referee!

Billy Thompson lived in Slaithwaite (pronounced 'Slouwit' by the locals) near to Huddersfield. One wintery Sunday my then Halifax team had an important league fixture against Oldham at Thrum Hall. We always met early Sunday morning and went through the afternoon's game plan. On arriving at the ground, I found it bone hard from the previous night's frost. Knowing Billy was the match official and that he lived not too far from Thrum Hall, I phoned his home and he duly came across the valley. We stood on the centre spot at the old ground and Billy asked, 'Do you want the game on Maurice?' Both Halifax and Oldham were going well and my side, after training on the pitch in training shoes, expressed a desire to play subject to Billy's decision. 'Okay, if it doesn't get any worse, we play,' declared Billy.

Oldham arrived at Thrum Hall one hour before kick off time. The players went straight out onto the frozen pitch and shook their heads at the state of the pitch. As they called to Billy that it was too hard, Billy approached and asked me, 'Well Maurice, do we play?' I answered in the affirmative and he called to the Oldham contingent, 'It's on'. Naturally we went inside and prepared for the game and I sent the late, great Stan Hardy, one of our kit men, to listen at the connecting door between the old dressing rooms to the Oldham conversation and report back to me.

Stan came back smiling, 'They took a vote and it went eight to seven to play'. I simply told the team that seven of the Oldham side did not want to play and all we had to do was to go about our business as usual. This we did and won the game 20 odd points to 10. The point is that I knew Billy liked his game of rugby as well as the fee from RLHQ for refereeing the game so my calculations were that Billy would play in an earthquake!

I can recount stories about most referees in the game and one story in particular involves the superb Fred Lindop, a referee I admired immensely. After being given the Leeds coaching job, my first game for the club was against Hull Kingston Rovers at Headingley in the second round of the John Player Trophy. Fred was the official in charge. I was carrying a £300 fine, suspended for 12 months, and time was still left on it. At half time, as I walked towards the dressing room, I checked on the penalty count and found out that Fred had 'murdered' us to the tune of 16 against and three for. Fred was just in front of me and I called to him in an irate manner, 'What about this penalty count Fred?' He turned and reminded me of my suspended fine.

Wanting to get my own back somehow, I said to the best referee of his day, 'If I called you a prat, what would you do?'

Fred said, 'I would remove you from the bench, report you to RLHQ and you would have to pay the £300'.

I waited a second and said, 'What if I thought you were a prat Fred?'

He walked on a pace and said, 'Well then I couldn't do anything about that'.

Just before we left the field I said, 'Well I think you are a prat!'

Despite our little argument Fred was still one of the better referees on the circuit. As we went into the period just before Super League, the Wigan twins, John and Robert Connelly came to the fore as did the former St Helens wingman, David Campbell, who indeed became a top cup final controller and an international referee. Stuart Cummings [Widnes], a Whitehaven lad, became the overall chief controller of referees and was a dominant figure as was Steve Cross [Hull] and John Holdsworth [Kippax] who attained international level. Amongst all these good referees, the outstanding one was the brilliant Russell Smith of Castleford. He was quick around the field as one would expect from a former wingman, he knew the game inside out and maintained his position as a top international referee through the years into Super League and was the top man in that era. Russell moved across the world to become a big league controller of games in the mighty NRL in Australia and his easy style and that superb quality of friendliness saw him maintain his high standard until his retirement from refereeing in 2006.

The referees mentioned in this chapter are the key referees from the breakaway in 1895 through to the other breakaway in 1995. A handful of Australians, New Zealanders and Frenchmen came into the game to officiate in the odd Test match or a few games before the Tests to acclimatise to our game prior to the big one. All brought a touch of the unusual to the supporters of the game. This chapter on referees was included to give an insight of what went on and what was said before, during and after some games in the good (and bad) old days. Obviously times and playing conditions were totally different from today. Referees didn't have the intensive scrutiny they have today, with the instant replays and slow motion TV shots, which tend to set up the referee for some pretty cheap shots from some regular TV callers. In a strange way the old format offered an unpredictability that is not there in today's game. Possibly today's younger supporters are watching the type of rugby league they like and want. Possibly, too, the referee, under an immediate microscope and wide open to verbal abuse, tends to provide a game that is very predictable these days. Who knows? Somewhere down the line we may produce another Reverend Frank Chambers or an Eric Clay or for that matter a Russell Smith. It would make a nice change and could well offer more unpredictability to the average spectator.

7

KIT AND KIT MEN

If you wanted to know anything that was going on in the club, then you asked the kit man! He knew everything about everything and everybody. Being a kit man meant that you joined the secret society of kit men. After games they would get together and exchange gossip, a bit like washerwomen. Generally they were a good bunch of men who were knowledgeable about the game. They had tips about getting grass stains out of white jerseys, matching up odd stockings and producing a pair as new, repairing draw strings in shorts (now that was a work of art) and cleaning the Vaseline jar so it sparkled compared to how it was left after the previous week's game. At some clubs it was his job to check the vital first aid box which accompanied all teams to all away games. In this box was a bottle of sol volatile, a jar of Vicks and a tube of 'Fiery Jack'. The sol volatile, mixed with water, was a vile substance that was supposed to ward off any sickness and settle one's stomach. The Vicks was pushed up one's nostrils to enable one to breathe better and rubbed into the chest and the Fiery Jack was avoided at all times except by the 'old heads' who rubbed it into their hands to smear across the face of an opponent in the tackle at the first opportunity.

Boots were usually the kit man's speciality. Training shoes, or pumps as they called them then, and spikes for sprint training all came within the kit man's scope. He checked and tightened studs in boots each Thursday evening when the coach gave the kit man his team to him to enable him to get out all the special paraphernalia that each player required. In the days prior to aluminium studs, which came over here from Australia with Arthur Clues, the studs were made of small leather rings and fastened to the sole of the boot by four long panel pins. The old kit men would gently pare off one ring of leather leaving the heads of the four pins just protruding below the stud. The boot then became lethal in the scrum or in the tackle. To be raked by these boots meant stitches at least. The new aluminium studs were, would you believe, deemed 'too dangerous' and originally banned. On their introduction every player finally used them and gashes on bodies reduced dramatically. These things did happen and they were the reason an equipment check was, and still is, carried out before each game.

Players needed protection as the game became more brutal. Hence there were knee pads, shin pads, shoulder pads, elbow pads, thigh pads and even back supports—a corset-like wraparound to give rigid support to some players who could not play without them. These items all became the responsibility of the kit man. If the weather had been hot and a downpour of rain had softened the ground the kit man would have with him a huge selection of long and short studs. Some players might ask for longer studs or shorter studs depending on the condition of the turf. The kit man would have with him his trusty stud key and have the old studs out and the new ones in swiftly. He would be at home games early to hang the playing jerseys, shorts and socks on each peg around the dressing room. Players were superstitious and liked to strip in the same place every week. The kit man learned where each player liked to change and had to be careful where to put the correct shorts. Many a time you would hear the stand off half or scrum half call out in anguish when the kit man had given them the wrong sized shorts. They would shout 'What the hell are these?' and stand there with a huge pair of shorts hanging from them causing their team mates to howl with laughter, 'Who do you think I am, Joe Smith [or some rotund player]?' they would shout amid the humour.

It depended on the wealth of each club as to how many helpers the kit man had. I played and coached at clubs who had several men buzzing around the dressing room pre-match and some clubs who had just the one. The kit man kept busy on match days right up to the time the team went out onto the field and during the game the kit man had spare kit handy if someone had his jersey or shorts torn. The kit man also carried out spare boots in a Hessian bag in case a player wasn't happy with his footwear for some reason. Immediately after a game at home or away the players always dropped their playing togs where they stripped. The kit man religiously picked up the jerseys first, then the shorts and finally the socks, counted them and turned each jersey to the playing side to check the number on its back. There had to be a correct tally before any player left the dressing room. If any item was missing the kit man made every player open his bag to see if a jersey or shorts or socks had found their way in there by 'mistake'. They always found the missing items. The away check was even more rigorous as some may well have, accidentally, swapped with a home player on the quiet. The condition of the footballs were the responsibility of the kit man too, as were the tackle bags and tackle shields which came in before Super League. New Mitre or Gilbert balls were kept for matches whilst much cheaper practice balls were used at training. This meant an almost daily check on the pressure inside the balls. Kit men were busy indeed.

On training nights at most clubs the kit was usually clean, dry and varied, with lots of different clubs' old jerseys on show. Australian, New Zealand and even French jerseys could be seen mixed among old club jerseys. The cagy kit man would secretly hand out this obsolete gear to his favourite players and there would be a mad scramble by the remaining players to grab what they could. This 'new' training gear, a basic jersey, shorts and socks had to last until players either brought their own training gear or waited for another 'hand out' by the kit man. Bearing in mind that a vast amount of training was done outdoors in winter, the attire to keep warm and dry was certainly not from the catwalks of Paris. There were odds and sods of track suits, woollen jumpers usually with big holes in them, two or three jerseys, 'Long Johns' worn under shorts, woolly hats and every kind of clothing that one could run in and keep dry. These were the days well before the jersey sponsorships of today. There was no specially designed training gear or modern waterproof suits. If a player wanted to lose a few pounds in weight he would cut holes in a plastic bag and wear the bag under his training gear.

Training in snow was always a fun thing. I used to devise team games in the snow, shuttle races pulling team mates along on plastic bags with six or seven in a team. The players loved the various exercises, all very strenuous, but supremely enjoyable. All snow sessions ended with the obligatory snowball fight. The Australian players adored these snow sessions. They stayed out after training building snow men and rolling around in the stuff, great fun! Of course the kit men hated the snow as it made hard work of preparing the kit for the next training session.

Depending on the financial standing of the club, the kit man's laundry was his pride and joy. Industrial washer-dryers were installed at some clubs and some even had special drying rooms where the gear was made bone dry from Tuesday to Thursday. But of course not all clubs were as well off or as organised as, say, Leeds where I coached on two different occasions. Headingley had a purpose-made laundry and two local ladies did the washing and drying each Wednesday and Monday resulting in spotlessly clean and dry kit every training night. On the other side of the coin, when I coached at Halifax in the late 1970s the club was down at heel. No hot water was available for our kit man because the heating had been cut off. The dressing room attendant then, John Kelly, had to wash the kit by hand in cold water and hang the washing up to dry in the cold wash room in the old pavilion. The players, on occasion, actually put on damp kit to play games in. The game, then, definitely was one of the haves and have nots. At Thrum Hall, when I first arrived as coach, there was only one set of decent blue and white hooped jerseys in the club. The 'A' team played in a sewn up, tatty set of ancient red and white jerseys which were, in fact, the first team's away strip. Thank goodness our blue and white hoops never clashed with our opponents' kit until we gained some new jerseys. Whilst the 'A' team strip was sewn together now and again, both the club's sides had only the one strip to play in. The 'A' team luckily played all their fixtures on Friday evenings under lights and the first team played on Sundays. This gave John Kelly Saturday to wash and dry the complete strip for the following day without heat.

Halifax had a super kit man in Stan Hardy. Playing with the 'A' team at Castleford one winter's Friday evening, the floodlights failed in a power cut half way through the first half. Stan was always in charge of the 'money bag' holding the players' wallets, rings, gold chains and loose cash. In the pitch black of the dressing rooms, as one by one the players left the large bath, Stan doled out the contents of the 'money bag'. He then put the bag on what he thought was the table but unfortunately turned out to be the bath! Someone found a 'tilly' lamp which illuminated the players as they groped around in the bottom of the bath with pound notes and the occasional fiver stuck to their backsides. Luckily everyone retrieved their property. When I coached at Huddersfield, I was more than a little surprised when going out to train one Tuesday evening. There on the field I saw 15 of my players dressed to the nines in the pristine jerseys, shorts and socks of another well known professional club. After doing a bit of Sherlock Holmes work I found out that one of our players had 'borrowed' the wicker skip from the boot of the other team's bus and doled out the full set of gear to train in. The same evening I had the gear individually wrapped and notified the other club that their gear had been dumped at our ground. They collected it, skip and all, the following day and we heard no more about it. The borrowing player was left in no doubt as to his further behaviour whilst at the club.

When I was a young player, I always treated kit men with the utmost respect. I realised that they had the power of making your football life either heaven or hell. My first professional club, Hull FC, were an upmarket club, well organised and well run. With respect to Dewsbury, the club I was transferred to, the surroundings were totally different.

Crown Flatt was an old ground, hardly changed from the Northern Union days. The kit room was approached via the home or first team dressing room and had a 'stable door' with the top half always open and the bottom half always locked. The kit man was a real old fashioned character, George Sharples, who had played for Dewsbury, on the wing, in the Challenge Cup final of 1912. George, for some reason, took to me and looked after me by giving me good kit. He was a grand elderly Lancastrian who still had the north west counties twang to his voice. He could be a little awkward to those he did not trust and only made one bad mistake in his entire kit man career. Legend in the Dewsbury dressing room was of a young, tough player who had been highly recommended to the Dewsbury club. The player arrived at the ground to train with a view to being signed that evening. George was waiting behind his 'stable door' and as the youngster asked for some training gear the old wingman snapped, 'Are you good enough to play for this club?' The young player expected a better greeting, turned around, went straight to Hull Kingston Rovers and signed for them. His name was Derek 'Rocky' Turner. When I returned to Dewsbury as 'A' team coach,

George had passed away and the kit man was another George, George Davies, who was brought up at the ground as his father had played there for many years.

When I was the 'A' team coach at Odsal, I worked with the Bradford Northern kit man, Fred Robinson. Fred was a great character, one of the old school. He knew every nook and cranny of the vast Odsal complex and every trick of the kit man's trade. One of Fred's assets was that he could keep a secret. He was a staunch supporter of his long time senior coach, Peter Fox and was Peter's kit man when the experienced Fox was the Great Britain coach. As we organised ourselves at Halifax, I built a purpose made boot room with pigeon hole shelving for training gear and boots, each with the player's name on it. I also asked two lifelong supporters, the late, great Stan Hardy and big Phil Coventry, if they would act as kit men. That was in 1977 and Phil Coventry is still there at the time of writing.

At Bramley on both occasions that I was senior coach, I had as kit man the late and sadly missed Keith Roberts. Keith and I played in the same junior side as kids at Headingley for the Leeds Juniors. Keith was a great hoarder of gear. Again I set up a proper boot room in the old McLaren Field dressing rooms and the gear Keith stashed away in the new cupboards was unbelievable. Keith also had the great kit man's ability of finding out things that were happening not only at Bramley but throughout the league! One had to be a wee bit careful in what you told Keith as there were three forms of communication at Bramley, telephone, television and tel Keith. All the same he was a good and thrifty kit man. At Headingley our kit man was a super bloke, the late Barry Adgie who again had been with us as kids at the Headingley Boys Club. The Headingley Boys Club housed the three youth teams of the Leeds club in premises on which now stands the Leeds Supporters Club behind the South Stand. In my first spell at the club, Billy Watts another great stalwart of the back room staff assisted Barry. At the time of writing, Billy is the Leeds club's official timekeeper.

My Great Britain kit man was Brian Cartwright who was groundsman at the Elland Road Stadium and chief setter out of pitches on football grounds for the Rugby Football League. Brian was the eternal optimist where the game was concerned up to his death a couple of years ago. The other kit men in the league were usually long time workers for their clubs. A cracking kit man who passed away recently was my old mate at another of the clubs I served, Prescot. Maurice Oldfield (Mo) was another of the old school who loved rugby league and all it stood for. The kit men throughout the league served the game as well as any international player or coach. They were the unsung heroes who put in long hours at their clubs mainly for the love of the club and the game.

Virtually everything regarding kit has changed during the 100 winters up to Super League. Referees progressed from wearing frock coats, knickerbockers and bowler hats, to wearing heavy navy blue blazers, complete with Society badge and long blue shorts. In the time of Eric Clay, a waterproof type outfit of black zipped up wind cheater and black shorts was introduced. This was very smart indeed. Then the fashion was fluorescent jerseys and for a short period, a vertical black and white striped jersey, not unlike the Newcastle United strip. Currently the vogue is for a pastel shade of a full strip, jersey and shorts, very chic indeed.

Playing strips and club colours have altered out of all recognition too. Certain clubs' jerseys were immediately recognised almost from day one. Hull FC's super irregular black and white hoops always looked smart and the immaculate claret and gold of the majestic Huddersfield would always guarantee fast, flowing football. Some clubs played in the same colours. Leigh, Oldham and Wigan all played in a red and white hooped jersey but each had its own identifying tag, for instance Oldham played in black shorts, Leigh in blue shorts and Wigan's jerseys at one time had wider hoops. Some clubs changed their traditional strips at some time or other, possibly in or just after the Second World War as all materials were in short supply. For instance Leeds changed their famous blue jersey with the irregular amber bands around chest and arms, to tangerine jerseys and blue shorts in their Wembley run of 1947. In the 1908 season they played in blue and yellow quartered jerseys with blue shorts and at various times in their history played in white jerseys, blue jerseys and green jerseys. In the 1936 Challenge Cup final at Wembley, Leeds played with blue collars and cuffs and blue shorts. Near neighbours Hunslet played, at times in their history, in chocolate and white jerseys and white shorts but the club's most famous colours were myrtle, flame and white with white shorts.

Of course the material of the jerseys has changed over the years. At the breakaway in 1896, jerseys were made of knitted wool with the shorts of hard wearing course twill, usually long enough to cover the knees. Later the jerseys were produced from a tough cotton twill as were the shorts and this type of material was used for many years until the early 1990s when the current material, a kind of nylon-polyester mixture, was accepted and all clubs began using this lighter, easier to handle material. Designs were no longer woven into the jersey but instead printed onto the jersey. Many traditional designs and colours were discarded as the old winter game turned, slowly at first, to embrace the new era of summer rugby. A few clubs have stayed true to their old traditions but quite a lot moved to different club jersey designs and have recently returned to something akin to former colours.

In the 100 winters' era, I remember as a kid watching with awe the Rochdale Hornets side play in colourful alternate red, white and blue hoops. The strangest strip, to the schoolboys in the juniors pen, was the Liverpool Stanley gear. They wore bright yellow jerseys with a big letter 'S' on the front and a white number on the back with white shorts. The three clubs in red and white were mentioned

Batley's wonderful 1897 Challenge Cup winning team

The man who changed the face of rugby, H.H. (Harry) Waller, the first chairman of the Northern Union

The great Harold Wagstaff— 'Prince of Centres'

Johnny Rogers, Billy Batten, Jonathan Parkin—three rugby league greats

Halifax—first ever Championship winners in 1907

Huddersfield Team of all talents (1914–15). Harold Wagstaff is behind Rosenfeld (with ball)

Wakefield Trinity's excellent 1948–49 team

Barrow and Great Britain player, Bill Burgess

Albert Rosenfeld, still the record try scorer in a season

The Great 'Bev'. Brian Bevan, the Warrington and Blackpool Borough wonder wingman

Sergeant Major Eric Clay in his pomp

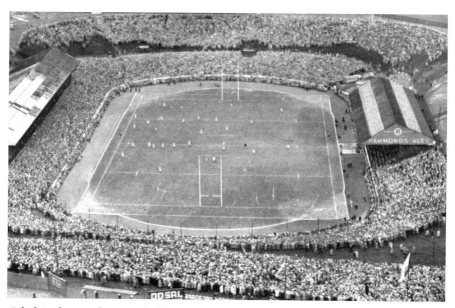

Odsal Stadium with a crowd of 102,000

Alan Hardisty lifts the John Player Trophy for Leeds

The great AGM, Alex Murphy

Billy Boston in full flight at Odsal

Alan Prescott accepts the Challenge Cup

The famous George Hotel, Huddersfield

Great Britain Lions, 1946

That great gentleman, Trevor Foster of Bradford Northern presents Barry Tyler to the Lord Mayor

Eddie Waring, TV personality, broadcaster and RL journalist

Two great rugby league men, Harry Jepson and John Holmes

The 'Black Pearl' Ellery Hanley breaks against Australia ©RLphotos.com

earlier: Oldham, red and white; Leigh, cherry and white; and Wigan, cherry and white but as mentioned, Wigan's hoops were broader. The teams would wear alternative jerseys when these clubs met and all three wore a blue jersey. St Helens and Hull Kingston Rovers wore identical jerseys, white with a red band and white shorts. Halifax carried the distinctive blue and white hooped jersey and white shorts, whilst Swinton played in navy blue jerseys, later blue with a white 'V' and white shorts. Barrow wore royal blue jerseys and white shorts and Bradford Northern wore those magnificent white jerseys with the single narrow red, amber and black band across the chest and arms. Dewsbury never altered their colours of alternate red, amber and black hoops with black shorts. Featherstone Rovers changed from chocolate and white to the famous blue with narrow white bands jersey with blue shorts. Bramley originally played in black jerseys and white shorts but changed later to amber and black jerseys with white shorts. Castleford wore amber and black and black shorts and Keighley had white jerseys and blue shorts but later changed to blue and white hoops and again to white jerseys with a scarlet and emerald green 'V' and white shorts. The famous 'Red Devils' of Salford carried the red jersey and white shorts, York wore amber and black with white shorts and Wakefield Trinity had the blue jersey with a broad red band and white shorts. Warrington sported the famous primrose and blue jersey with white shorts and Widnes had broad black and white hoops with white shorts. Workington Town wore a white jersey with a blue band and white shorts. Whitehaven supported a white jersey with chocolate, blue and gold bands and white shorts. Doncaster had white jerseys with blue and gold bands and white shorts. Sheffield Eagles wore white, claret and gold jerseys with white shorts.

Many teams have come and gone since the breakaway but the few who stayed for a while included Broughton Rangers who wore navy blue jerseys with white shorts, St Helens Recreation wearing red, amber and black with white shorts and the London club Streatham and Mitcham who wore green and white hoops with white shorts. Huyton who had evolved from Wigan Highfield to London Highfield to Liverpool City via Liverpool Stanley and later became Runcorn Highfield and later still, Prescot, played in black jerseys with a red collar and black shorts. Chorley Borough, formerly Blackpool Borough, Springfield Borough, Lancashire Lynx and back to Blackpool wore black jerseys with white shorts. As Blackpool they wore black jerseys with a green shoulder patch and black shorts. Carlisle carried blue jerseys with a red and white band and white shorts. Cardiff City, then Bridgend, both played in blue jerseys with a yellow 'V' and blue shorts. Southend Invicta formerly Kent Invicta wore a white jersey with a blue 'V' and white shorts. Fulham, who went on to become London Crusaders, London Broncos and Harlequins RL, had black jerseys with a red and white 'V', black shorts and Mansfield Marksmen, light and dark blue jerseys and blue shorts.

Sponsorships took control of many traditional club jerseys with all sorts of products mentioned on the front of strips. As Great Britain coach I was called to a meeting to air my views on an offered sponsorship from Batchelor's Foods. I shrank back in horror as the Chief Executive read out the terms of the offered deal. On the front of the Great Britain jersey the company wanted 'Batchelor's Mushy Peas'! Our game, no doubt because of its northern image, has always been a target for beer and cigarette manufacturers. The game accepted sponsorships from them initially but with the ban on cigarette advertising and the bad publicity of drunkenness recently, the bigger clubs, with their Sky Sports TV exposure, are being sponsored by more of a 'family' orientated group of sponsors. In the space of a few short years we have main sponsors' logos emblazoned across jerseys, minor sponsors' miniature emblems on jersey sleeves, shorts and even stockings. Everything is considered in the sponsorship stakes including the old yarn about teams being sponsored by Tampax, especially those going through a bad period!

Not too long ago, the actual football sponsorship was held by Mitre Sports of Huddersfield, who provided 20 new rugby balls per season per club. Then the famous football manufacturers, Gilbert, joined the rugby league as sponsors and now there are several companies whose product is kicked and passed around all the grounds in all divisions of our game, Steeden and Puma to name but two. The footballs have changed over the years too. Now they are standardised, the only difference on the balls is the various makers' highly decorative markings and of course the maker's name. In the old days, some balls were as round as soccer balls, others were long and narrow. It was almost impossible to allow for which way these long narrow balls would bounce, the normal ball will always find you out if allowed to bounce but this type of ball was deadly. Some were as slippery as glass others as rough as sandpaper. Now all are the same, which tends to make for easier and safer handling throughout the season.

The kit used so long ago is now an amusing memory. But things in football and in life generally have a habit of returning and one or two clubs have changed back into kit resembling their old style design. As the clubs now follow the soccer vogue of changing designs annually to make more money from admiring supporters, the old favourite colours may once again be seen on many grounds as in the past.

8

SIGNING AND TRANSFERRING PLAYERS—AND THE BACKHANDERS

To change one's club in the old days was a straightforward and easy operation. A player would tell, verbally or in writing, his club secretary that he wished to join another club and all he had to do was wait until the new club's secretary received a courtesy letter. If the mail was late the player would simply turn out for his new club with a word to the referee before the game kicked off. Soon after the 1895 breakaway in 1898–99, the first season of open and accepted professionalism, the registration of players was introduced. This called for each player to be registered with the secretary of the new union and a player could only be transferred if all the proper terms and agreements were drawn up and lodged with the union secretary. This was a much better organised, more professional system than previously.

The systems of signing and transferring players, from the breakaway through the 100 years to the advent of Super League, before the Bosman ruling, in professional rugby league was archaic. For many years individual contracts for set periods were unusual to say the least. When signing for a professional club, one normally signed for a full career. The procedure for signing a youngster was that the player should be at the legal age to sign. This legal age altered over the years. When I signed as a professional player in 1953, the legal age was 16 and had been younger previously. Sometimes a player was 'spotted' by a club scout and invited to play trial games at the club. Usually the player was asked to play three trial games at the end of which either the player was released or a monetary offer was made again, usually via a standard club 'contract'. This contract was an agreement to sign for that club for a figure, this figure paid over a period of time at so much on signing and the remainder of the agreed figure paid at the start of each season until the agreed figure was paid in full. This figure was officially tax free as, if signing from amateur football, it was paid to the player for relinquishing his amateur status. No further money, under no circumstances, was allowed to be paid to a player who had received a signing on fee previously. This was rugby league law.

Once signed, the player belonged to that club and could legally be sold on to another club, transferred, for as much money as possible, but still could not, officially, be paid a penny piece for the move. Nor was the buying club allowed to speak to the player without the selling club's permission. If clandestine meetings were held between the buying club and player then this was deemed as an 'illegal approach' and the buying club was heavily fined. So if a club signed a youngster, say for £500, and a few seasons later the player had developed into a good professional, they could transfer him to another club, for say £5,000, £10,000 or £30,000. Officially the player would be expected to move for absolutely nothing! A player was rewarded if he had 10 years unbroken service to one club, by being able to apply to the RFL for a benefit season. If granted, the player had to form his own benefit committee and could, if he worked his socks off, earn a substantial sum but when divided by 10 it was still only a token amount for all those years of loyalty. Some clubs did show a semblance of gratitude to the player by allowing him to move on in a 'free transfer' to another club in appreciation of his services, but these cases were few and far between. There were several cases of players 'outsmarting' the club's directors who showed a mercenary tendency where 'free transfers' were concerned.

The famous and brilliant player, Jonathan 'Jonty' Parkin, was one of those clever players. Jonty signed for Wakefield Trinity in 1913 as an 17 year old and soon became a renowned and brilliant player. He represented Great Britain on 17 occasions, making three tours to Australia and New Zealand, twice as captain. He was awarded a benefit game in 1922 against Leeds on account of receiving only a small signing on fee. This benefit game produced a figure of £700— a small fortune then. The international selectors considered him too old for the first Test match against Australia in 1929 and at the age of 35 years old left him out of the team. The Aussies won the Test 31– 8 and Jonty was hurried back into the team for the second and third Tests. Great Britain won them both. It was sad but the Wakefield committee considered Jonty too old for them too and decided to transfer list him at £100. Quick as a flash, Jonty bought himself and became a free agent, this made him legally able to sign on again for anyone and claim a signing on fee. This he did for Hull Kingston Rovers, for considerably more than the £100 he paid for himself.

Transfer fees would fluctuate depending on the quality of player and there have been several unusual fees paid for players. One club, who were having extensive alterations to their ground, swapped a player for a second hand turnstile which they fitted into the new alterations. Another unusual transaction was by Rochdale Hornets with Dewsbury. The Hornets were interested in a second row forward playing at Crown Flatt, so the story goes. They watched him several times but were undecided whether to sign him. They went to watch him one final time in a Dewsbury home game and decided not to sign him but instead bought the snooker table which had for years been used, covered with boards and a table cloth, as the food table in the Dewsbury player's tea room. Legend has it that the table played for years for Hornets in the second row. It was very slow but took some knocking down in the tackle!

Player swaps were fairly common and a deal that involved money and a player for a player were regularly done. Many times the player involved with the money plus player deal, considered not worth keeping by the swapping club, came good at his new club and usually haunted his former club with great performances. Some clubs were genuine in their attempts to allow a player to move on. In the late 1970s, whilst coaching at Halifax, I enquired at Wakefield Trinity about the availability of a former junior scrum half of mine in amateur football, Terry Langton. A tough competitor, Terry was struggling to keep a first team place at Belle Vue and I agreed a deal of £750 to buy him. The deal was £250 paid over three seasons. What a bargain Terry was as he was a good half back. Wheeling and dealing was an art in days gone by, especially at the less fashionable clubs with little money to spend. There were some very streetwise characters in the game then and one had to 'get up early', as they used to say, to get the best of a deal.

This little anecdote tells of the type of things one had to do to get one's man. I was coaching at the grand old club, Bramley, and fancied the Keighley back rower, Alan Clarkson, to partner a young, newly signed kid, Karl Harrison, in my second row. I knew the Keighley coach well and contacted him about the availability of Clarkson. 'Oh, you'll need a lot of money to buy him,' gloated the Keighley coach. He then went on about wanting one of my old players at Halifax, Dave Cholmondley. Halifax had on loan from Bramley a player whom they wanted but we at Bramley didn't. After speaking to the Keighley coach I phoned Ken Roberts the then Halifax coach and did a deal for the Bramley loan player in a straight swap for Dave Cholmondley. I explained to Dave that I would only want him for a short while but would get him a few quid from Bramley and a lot more from another club, not named. Once I had Dave in the safe, I phoned the Keighley coach and asked him if he still fancied Dave. 'He would just slot into my side perfectly,' he told me.

'How much do you value Clarkson at?' I asked him.

'Oh, much more than you can afford.'

I waited a second, then said, 'I have Dave Chum'. Silence on the phone. Then all the names under the sun came flooding down the line. 'Here's the deal,' I said to the other coach, 'we swap players and you find a good lump for Chum.' He agreed and the deal was done. It was not always as easy as that!

The term 'good lump' indicated a 'backhander'. This was a payment to an incoming player in lieu of an official payment, a bung, which was against all the laws of the Rugby Football League. In the early days of the Northern Union and before that, there were 'gifts' handed over to the player one wanted to sign. A length of cloth, a trouser length, a suit, a gold crown hidden in a player's boot, an envelope pushed through the letter box at night, all were ways that players were given a 'bung' for playing for this or that club.

Some outrageous backhanders were asked for, amounts of money that no club would pay, and there were some players who made a very good 'nest egg' by moving about to plenty of clubs, big and small. One of these players was the late Geoff Clarkson, a tough back rower, who went almost all over the league in a career that saw him gain a Wembley winner's medal with Leigh in 1971 and various winners' trophies with Bradford Northern. Geoff was a nice, friendly bloke off the field but a highly motivated competitor on the meadow. He liked the winning money. I remember big Geoff once telling me when we worked at Bramley together, 'When I came from rugby union, I came because of the money and nothing has changed'. His clubs were Wakefield Trinity twice in 1966 and 1978, Bradford Northern twice in 1968 and 1980, Leigh twice in 1970 and 1981, Warrington 1971, Leeds 1972, York 1975, Bramley 1976, Hull

Kingston Rovers 1978, Oldham 1980 and Featherstone Rovers 1983. Geoff was 40 years old when he last played in first team rugby.

The most honest and straight forward backhander I was ever involved with was when coaching Huddersfield. I went with the chairman to see a former international loose forward at his home and after polite conversation the question of his backhander arose. Taking the bull by the horns I said, 'Right, how much will it cost us to get you to Fartown?'

The player didn't hesitate, 'I will need £232.25p', he said. Both the chairman and I were dumfounded. I, for one, was expecting much more than that and so was the chairman. The player went on, 'You see we have just had a new bathroom fitted and that amount I have asked for is the estimate the tiler has just sent me'. He was an honest man and a damned good player as well as cheap!

Ronnie Dobson was a good friend who gave me my second chance as a coach in first team professional football. Ronnie and I went out to a hotel between Castleford and Pontefract to talk to a good stand off half who was in dispute with his club. At the time Ronnie was the football director at Halifax and I had advised him of this player's availability. The player could play at loose forward and in the centre so he would have been an excellent signing for us at Thrum Hall. Over a pint we got down to brass tacks. Ronnie opened the bidding when he asked how much the player was looking for. 'I want £2,000 in my hand, £2,000 at Christmas this year and £4,000 at the end of the season.' Ronnie nearly choked on his pint as the player's demands seeped into his brain. We were in the old second division but aspired to be promoted that season so we were buying for the first division.

'And is that it?' asked a spluttering Ronnie, knowing full well that we were not getting that much money through the turnstiles for two home games.

The player sensed the tension in Ronnie's voice and said, 'I can always take a grand now and £7,000 at the end of the season.'

Ronnie gestured with a nod towards the door, put on his overcoat and said, shaking hands with the player, 'We'll let you know'. We never saw the player again.

Players had a regular time for intimating the amount of backhander they wanted. The two clubs would agree a transfer figure, then the player was informed that he would be joining the buying club. Then the player would talk to the buying club and try to screw as much as he could from them. Many times the deal was scrapped because the player would not budge from his required 'bung'. Some selling clubs pulled out of deals because the player asked them for a bung to leave. A few did give a bung if they were strapped for cash but most said, 'Stay here and rot'.

The Leeds club, unbelievably as straight as a die, had a unique way of getting players they wanted and still managed to keep their books dead straight. They would find out via the selling club what the player was looking for to join them. Say the selling club had agreed to a selling fee of £20,000 and the player wanted say £2,000 for himself, then Leeds would offer a revised fee of £21,000 and let the selling club offer the player £1,000 bung and if needed negotiate the other £1,000 themselves. In that case the Leeds club books were spotless. Some chairmen arranged with their board to begin a 'sludge fund', filtering a few quid each home game from the 'gate'. This sludge fund paid out the bungs for new players.

A favourite trick of some of the richer clubs was to contact the player they wanted secretly and find out how much he wanted to join them. The club told the player that they would make an offer for him in a straight transfer deal but if his club would not play ball then the player was advised by the buying club to 'stay away' from training and playing and they would pay his wages that he lost. Many clubs have let players go after a short time of staying away. Cash plus a player was another method clubs used to get the man they wanted.

The player in this deal was called a 'makeweight'. This deal was usually done between a rich club and a not so rich club. The rich club might want a good player from the poorer club. The money offered may not reach the value put on the player by the poor club so a makeweight was suggested. If the poorer club could swing it to get the makeweight then they usually did well out of the deal as the player joining them nearly always became one of their better players. For years the smaller clubs had to sell their better players to balance the books and many lads have saved their parent club by agreeing to move on to pastures greener.

Transfer fees in rugby league have never touched the incredible heights of the Football League payments. From our game breaking away from rugby union in 1895, it took 16 years for the first £1,000 transfer fee to be paid. This was when Leeds paid Hunslet £1,000 in the 1921–22 season for signing the fine player Harold Buck. In 1901–02 season Jimmy Lomas was sold from Bramley to Salford for £100. Nine years later Jimmy was sold to Oldham for £300. Then in 1912–13 the great Billy Batten went from Hunslet to Hull FC for the magnificent sum of £600. One of the strangest transfers was that of the late Ike Southward in 1958–59 from Workington Town to Oldham for £10,650. This beat the previous record the season after Mick Sullivan was transferred from Huddersfield to Wigan for £9,500. Then in 1960–61 Mick Sullivan went to St Helens from Wigan for £11,000 to recover the record fee but that same season Workington Town bought Ike Southward back from Oldham for a new record fee of £11,002-10 shillings.

There have been one or two cases of youngsters signing from junior football for more than one club. Of course it wasn't long before the Rugby Football League noticed this anomaly and refused to accept all registrations except the first one. Such was the case of the very good international centre, the late Keith Holden. He was a junior whiz kid from local rugby union. He had everything, size, pace and a footballing brain. He signed for Leigh and then for Wigan. The RFL HQ saw this and refused to accept his registration for either of the clubs until the player sorted out the problem. In the meantime Keith trained with Swinton who for some reason thought that he would sign for them but Keith's dad came to the rescue with sound common sense and the lad signed for Leigh. He later signed for Wigan, then Oldham, on to Warrington, back to Wigan and finally to Blackpool Borough.

The registration of players was a relatively easy business but problems for the administration arose in Australia in 1947 with the 'residential rule' which brought into being the law that made every player play for the area in which he officially lived. There were ways around this as worked by Western Suburbs 'Magpies', where the then secretary, Lou Moses, had 11 players listed as supposedly living with him at his Croydon, Western Suburbs address.

The Wigan club raised a few eyebrows in 1991–92 when they signed the exciting wing three quarter, Martin Offiah from Widnes for a massive £440,000 giving an idea how finances of some clubs had improved and inflation had risen since the move by Jimmy Lomas in 1901–02 for £100. Now the players' contract system is firmly in place, the original transfer system has become outdated. It is still used occasionally if a player changes clubs whilst still in contract. The old transfer system is sadly missed, in a way, as money moving around the clubs via transfers was, in some cases, the thing that allowed some clubs to make ends meet. The second occasion I coached Leeds, I was involved twice in a few months in record breaking transfer deals in 1987–88. Both deals were with Hull FC and one deal was when buying the young international forward, Lee Crooks, from Hull FC for £150,000, then to Hull FC again for the grand footballer, Garry Schofield, for £155,000.

Almost every club in the league paid some sort of backhander if they really wanted a player. Hardly any were ever 'caught' and every man and his dog at Rugby League HQ knew this was going on but turned a blind eye to it. The Inland Revenue would have been most interested in the backhanders but clubs were smart and covered their tracks.

Signing an overseas player was totally different to signing a local player. Firstly the player from abroad was usually signed on a short contract, say one or two seasons in duration as opposed to the local player who was signed until he retired, was transferred or released. Some overseas players signed for longer periods but usually they were deemed as 'not required' by an overseas club. Suddenly round about the late 1970s and early 1980s, all kinds of restrictions were placed on overseas players, mainly because of the new social justice feeling that players were coming over and our local players were not being given the chance. I can see sense in that but at the time of coaching Leeds, we were notified that before we signed the great wing three quarter from Australia, Eric Grothe, we had to advertise the fact that we were looking for an international class wingman in the local Job Centre in Headingley. A card was placed in the window of the Job Centre which read:

Wanted

An experienced wing three quarter to play in the Rugby Football League's first division. The applicant must stand 6 feet or over, be a minimum of 14 stones in weight, have an accepted running measured speed of 14 seconds for the distance of 100 yards, must be a regularly recorded scorer of tries in the club's level of participation, be fit and strong enough to fulfil the requirements of the club's coach and physiotherapist and be able to produce references to support his application. Contact: The Secretary, Leeds RLFC, The Pavilion, Headingley Grounds, Leeds 6.

We received three local applications, one came from an ex

professional who had played for Liverpool City quite a few years ago and fulfilled all criteria but was 48 years old! Another application came from someone who had played in amateur rugby at a good county level but hadn't played for six seasons since having a quadruple heart bypass five years ago. The third applicant was a 20 year old student who, although never playing one game in his life, felt that he covered all the required needs the club was looking for except he was 5 feet 2 inches tall and weighed just over 8 stones but he added he was prepared to gain a few pounds to secure the position. We decided not to interview the applicants as the time factor for receiving the applications expired. As did the coach, almost!

The fees that overseas players attracted were exorbitant in those days and paid into offshore banks to eliminate any tax problem. If the player came for a two season spell then on top of the return air fare for him and sometimes his wife and kids he would want another air fare to go home and back in our summer between the two seasons for all the family. The player also needed a house renting in a plush area for the player and his family, and the family would need a good car providing as well as sometimes a job for the player's wife or girlfriend! A single player would only need all the return fare for one. The player of course was a full time professional but may, for a few quid more, come to work, how they hated this four letter word, on the ground staff at the club. A top class player coming to a top class club needed all these perks. What of the lesser or unknown player coming to a smaller club? Did he receive the same treatment? No, to be blunt, this player could expect a fair deal in most things that the top of the range player received but of a lesser standard. His money, for instance, would be paid weekly and taxed. This would be refunded on his departure from this country, if he was lucky. He would receive one return fare, his house would be in a working class area and he would need a job to supplement his much lesser signing fee and he would have no car. In those days car sponsorships were a thing of the future and hardly any club had a car deal in its short contracts, unless it was one of the top six clubs in a 30-odd team league.

At the time of the government's clamp-down on overseas players, during the advertising at the Job Centre syndrome, it was awkward to gain a working visa for overseas players stating that they were in this country specifically to play rugby league football. Even if a visa was issued it had to be word perfect with serial numbers and quoted references and all sorts of unusual paraphernalia relating to the club he was joining. Leeds signed an international front row forward and he flew into Manchester with everything in order, except for a serial number which was accidentally missing from the visa. On arrival he went towards Customs and was immediately arrested and put into a holding cell within the airport. I was contacted at Headingley and drove as quickly as possible over to Manchester to release our star signing. I took with me the secret password, the missing serial number, and was told that our man was about to be placed on the next flight to Sydney but upon producing the serial number, within 10 minutes the new prop and I were winging our way back to Leeds and normality.

The luck of the Aussies was with Eric Grothe and his family when they walked through the gate and into the Manchester Airport foyer on his entry into this country to play at Headingley. He was awarded a holiday in any European country for being the one millionth traveller on Qantas Airlines to England. As I have already said, the contract system gradually took hold in our game and by doing so siphoned most of the smaller clubs' money away. Little chance to recover the money through the transfer system as before, condemned the smaller clubs to withdraw from employing even the lesser paid overseas players. This seemed a shame because supporters of those clubs are denied the chance to watch one or two decent Aussies, Kiwis or South Sea Islanders. But the old game rolls on and it has seen wholesale changes since the fateful meeting at the George Hotel, ranging from fewer players on the field, the introduction of coaches to teach the teams, a huge amount of rule and law changes, flying across the world to play the game and players being full time and openly highly paid. Whatever happened to the 'trousers length' and 'six bob a day' days?

9

CHANGING
OUR GAME

As I have been involved in the game for many years, I have seen many changes take place in the laws and rules of the game, of the way the game is, and was, run, and in the changes in the basic principles that the old game attempted to achieve. There have been changes in attitudes between clubs, there was always a feeling of goodwill and clubs almost always helped each other when in difficulties. Speaking from a traditionalist's view, the awesome wrench in the turn to Super League and the advent of summer football must have been the biggest change by far. The chasm becomes wider every year between the haves and have nots as the top eight or nine teams in the big league become more established. The memory of the old game pre Super League refuses to go away, so highly esteemed was it and it is impossible not to compare the two games even though many may think that comparisons are futile.

Many rugby league experts, both male and female, still, after almost 14 years, cannot accept how Super League has changed the game they loved. Yet, in retrospect, one may say that it is only history repeating itself, as there is a similarity in the 1895 split and the 1995 change. Both were made for the betterment of such a simple game. Both brought a new aspect of thought and action to a game that, in fairness, was going nowhere. Both were stagnating and may well have died if drastic action had not been taken. At the breakaway in 1895 the efforts of several far sighted men were thwarted by the attitudes of the establishment of the old school tie brigade. They had been raised on the belief that the game of rugby football was devised for the minority of well to do young men who could afford to maintain their amateurism. The breakaway had to come. So too had the change over in 1995. If this had not occurred, with the assistance of the Sky TV contract, then so many clubs who were at their wits end financially could so easily have gone without a trace. The traditionalists would stand for some significant law and rule changes but drew the line at changing the whole concept, including the time and season of the year in which their beloved game was played. The whole game reeled back in disbelief when the concept of a Super League was unveiled. The majority did not know what to think of it and could not come to terms with such a huge change happening almost overnight. The original blueprint included clubs in near proximity to each other merging. Oh, catastrophe! 'Merge, never!' was the cry. There were silent demonstrations in town centres. In one demonstration in particular at Thrum Hall, Halifax, hundreds of supporters silently walked around the perimeter of the pitch at half time in a wonderfully organised silent protest against the proposed merger with the old 'enemy', Huddersfield. Looking back since the change, one wonders if that might not have been a good idea! The proposed mergers seemed to bypass the 'bigger' clubs and join together the 'smaller' clubs and this would not be accepted by the proletariat. So Super League was born, and with its birth the professional game changed without recognition.

Our initial game was staunchly embedded in the winter months. Early season was September, late season was April, lasting almost nine months including the Wembley Challenge Cup final and the end of season Championship play offs. The amateur game is still played in the winter months and although their season is little changed from the breakaway, their format has changed considerably. Traditional training sessions remain to be Tuesday and Thursday evenings. The sessions were usually performed outdoors, on the playing pitch in dry weather and in the grandstand or road running when wet. Because of the fierce winters we had then, games were postponed during the season because of frost or snow and the end of season had to be adhered to because of the Championship play offs. Some of these postponed games had to be fitted in mid week or on free weekends if both sides had been knocked out of the Challenge Cup. Teams could rearrange a postponed game for the cup tie weekend but many teams had a long run in to the season's end by playing Sunday and Wednesday until the backlog of fixtures was complete. If the away game involved a fair distance to travel, then the home team would make an early decision on the state of the pitch. Sometimes acrimonious feelings would arise between the two clubs' chairmen if a game was called off.

One such incident took place at Lawkholme Lane, Keighley in the winter of the 1979–80 season. I was coaching Halifax and we looked well placed for promotion. The fixture at Keighley was tricky as the late Alan Kellett, their coach, had the side playing well. I had a funny feeling about the game as it was one we could easily lose. The weather turned cold that week on Wednesday, with a slight thaw up to the early afternoon. Unfortunately, the frost returned with a vengeance from around 2.00pm. Our kick off time was 3.00pm and when we arrived at 2.00pm the turnstiles were open and spectators were entering the ground. The entrance fee was £1 at the time and we still had the old £1 notes as legal tender. My players and I went on to the field to see the state of the pitch—typical of all football pitches in our climate, it was playable in some parts but bone hard in others. The Keighley ground has a low lying stand opposite the main stand and the low stand threw a shadow the full length of the field for about a yard into the playing area. This area was like concrete. No sun had shone on this strip of field since the cold snap began. I, as coach, did not want to play at this time and when I saw my players digging their heels into the iron hard turf and shaking their heads ruefully I knew this was not our day. Mr Peter Massey was the referee and he walked around the ground with the Keighley chairman, who obviously wanted to play. This was because he and his board expected one of their better gates as both teams were playing well and this was a 'derby' game. By this time there must have been about 2,000 spectators settling in to see a rough house of a game. On the field were my football director, Ronnie Dobson and our experienced chairman Mr Bill Hughes. Mr Hughes whispered to me, 'Maurice, if we think it's too hard then we won't play'.

This suited me and I called over to Peter Massey to look at the concrete hard strip under the low stand. 'Sorry Peter but I'm not sending my team out to get injured on this pitch.'

The referee said, 'This strip of pitch is not playable. It's definitely too hard. But the Keighley chairman says that his groundsman can put the touchline a yard in and then I think it would be playable'.

'Oh dear,' I thought, 'act quickly, Maurice, or these two men will stitch you up!' 'That's okay by me,' I said, 'but if you do that then I'll ask that both sets of posts be moved 18' to make them central on the field of play.' I knew that they knew that this was impossible. The Keighley chairman, who also knew that he had made a bad mistake by opening the turnstiles before a decision was made on the safety of the pitch, fired a tirade of abuse and foul language at me, my team and my club. Mr Hughes my chairman, whose experience with the Halifax club was like a vast reservoir of laws and rules of the game, demanded an immediate apology, there and then, from his opposite chairman. He received one and gracefully retired from the field. Peter Massey sensibly called the match off stating it was 'Postponed because of the hardness of the pitch'. Most of the large crowd of spectators were incensed. They jeered and cat-called our team all the way back into the dressing room. The footnote to this story is that as we were returning to our team bus, the crowd were still filing out through the main gates of the ground. Three members of the ground staff with huge bundles of £1 notes stood by the main gates handing the entrance fee back to the supporters. Because of the crush, my team, my directors and I drifted past the people handing out £1 notes and we all had a note thrust into our hands! What a laugh we had on the way back to Halifax but when we went to the rearranged game, Ronnie Dobson made the team and coaches pay to get into the ground. That is what it was like in those days, anything could happen at a game and it usually did!

Communications had to be up to scratch in winter time to keep the visiting team in the picture as to the state of the ground. This meant that the people at the home ground had to be on the ball and the secretary had the job of making sure that the away team did not travel if the ground was unfit. In the winter of 1979 when I was at Halifax, we were drawn to play Wigan away in the Challenge Cup. We travelled to Central Park on the Sunday of the game only to find on arrival that the ground was rock hard and had been since the previous Thursday. Although Wigan were apologetic, the fact was that my Halifax team had no need to have travelled. The game was rearranged for the following Wednesday evening. The Halifax chairman, Mr Bill Hughes, himself a great secretary in years gone by, checked with Wigan mid afternoon on Wednesday and was told that the game was on. We set off again and arrived to find that the pitch was as bad as ever, bone hard with frost on top of the divots. I would have had more to say about it except the official who met us at Central Park was the famous player, Vince Karalius who, at the time, was Wigan coach. Vince explained that when the Wigan secretary had spoken to Mr Hughes the pitch was playable but at the time we set off from Halifax for the game, there was a sudden drop in temperature and an immediate frost. Within 90 minutes the

pitch was as hard as iron again. We had to make a third trip to
Central Park the following Wednesday evening and again had the
game snatched from us by the referee in the last minute by
disallowing a perfectly good try under the posts (I explained this in
greater detail in Chapter 6). One must remember that there were no
mobile phones then and if that incident had happened playing away
in Cumbria, then someone from Halifax would have jumped into
their car, chased the bus up the M6 and caught up with it around
half way there and turned us around. These unavoidable mistakes
only happened occasionally. To say we went from 1895 through the
early 1970s without motorways in the north there were few mistakes.

Before motorways, frost and snow played havoc with games, as
only the Leeds ground at Headingley had underground heating and
could, 99% of the time, be certain that a game would go on. Before
the 'electric blanket' at Leeds the favourite weapon against these
cold elements was straw. Bales of straw were stacked in many
grounds as autumn turned to winter. On the threat of a cold spell
from the meteorological office, the ground staff would lay the golden
coloured straw all over the pitch to a depth of around 18 inches to
2 feet. It would be all hands to the pumps to get the straw down as
it was a big job to do by hand. The logistics of removing it to play
were of a horse of a vastly different colour. It took more manpower
to move it than was needed to put the stuff down. Timing was of the
essence. The pitch had to be ready to play for a 2.30pm kick off and
the pitch had to be marked out and generally tided up for just before
the start. There were no floodlights then and on a mid-winter
evening as the game ended, night approached fast. The straw had to
be replaced but this time it was different to the dry golden stuff that
had been laid the first time. Now it was dirty, heavy, wet and it broke
one's back when lifted so that an operation that took one lift and
drop originally now took several lifts and movements to cover and
protect the ground. The manpower needed came from supporters

who were asked around Wednesday in the local newspaper, to come early on Saturday, in rain, snow or blow to clear the straw to the sides of the pitch. I can never remember any game failing to start at Leeds. Taking off the straw and replacing it in the light of large gas burners was a masterpiece of organisation. On arrival schoolboys and adults were formed into gangs, about 10 people per gang and each gang had one shovel and two wheelbarrows. There was a supervisor for each gang, usually one of the ground staff and each gang was designated an area of the pitch. The straw was stacked all around the pitch against the perimeter fence or wall, with room for the touch judges to run on the outside of the playing area. The supervisor released the helpers just before kick off time and told them where to meet up after the game to re-lay the straw. For their labour the volunteers received free entry to the game and a half a crown when the supervisor took them up to the secretary's office on completion of the task. The organised gangs started removing the straw around 12.30pm and the re-laying took around an hour after the game. As a kid the 2s. and 6d. was secondary to the bragging rights one had at school on Monday morning.

In the early days clubs would use a series of coal or wood burning braziers, set in lines up and down the field and tended from early morning of the game until kick off time. There was a quick clean up of fire debris and the match was on. One Widnes company gave the club a chemical that kept frost at bay but destroyed the turf where used. The preparation of the playing area, after a snow fall or deep frost, was, over the years, made easy through experience. The police safety orders on a ground did not care about playing the game they worried more about spectators. After a heavy snow fall sometimes games were called off by the police because of deep snow on the actual terraces of the grounds. Ground staff made great efforts to clear the terraces and the police would allow huge piles of cleared snow to be situated in the corners of the terraces so long as they were cordoned off. Games were allowed to continue in a snow storm and the ground staff could be seen clearing the touchlines, try lines and dead ball lines with 2 foot wide scrapers and a mate following, marking out the lines in blue dye so that they could be seen through the snow. On occasion the ground staff would wait until play was deep in one half then quickly dash across field to clear and remark in blue the far '25' line across the field, then the same at the other end. The half way line was completed at half time. I remember playing, coaching and watching in snow storms. In one game at Oldham the referee told both teams to stop moaning and get on with the game as a blizzard hit the Watersheddings. It was impossible to see the old double decked stand at the bottom of the field through the snow blowing up the slope.

When coaching in amateur football, we played at Crigglestone in a cup tie. Their ground looked like the end of the earth with a huge snow storm blowing across the valley and the pitch situated on the top of a hill. It was impossible to see a yard in front but the intrepid referee played on. One of the worst snow storms I saw was in one of the rounds of the Challenge Cup in February 1957 when the storm arrived mid way through the Leeds versus Warrington cup tie. How the game was finished I will never know as it was a whiteout, ground staff constantly clearing lines and players unrecognisable. But finish they did and what an exciting game it was in between the gusts of the storm.

Often the conditions won, despite heroics from spectators attempting to clear pitches and terraces. I coached at a club that had more matches postponed than any other, Halifax. When the snow came to Halifax it was like being in Alaska. I remember one particular storm that drifted snow up the slope of the old Thrum Hall ground. As we stood before the drift with our barrows and shovels at the ready, the snow—no exaggeration—was 5 feet deep. I honestly thought we would never play at the old ground again. Of course after the snow came the floods and waterlogged pitches. New

Hunslet, as they were then, played for a spell at the Greyhound Stadium at Elland Road. In one cup tie against Warrington on the tight little ground with the 'tuning fork' posts, the American Grid Iron type, New Hunslet hired a helicopter to hover above the pitch to dry out the flooded pitch and it worked! Sometimes pitches were so muddy that the teams had to change their jerseys at half time so that the referee could recognise the teams and players.

Recently the Super League was caught in a cold, wet, spell of weather as they played their one-off Boxing Day warm up games. The uproar from the press, about subjecting these athletes to such atrocious conditions, made me and other old timers, I'm sure, smile as one thought of the three matches in three days we played in and over Christmas. The Christmas Day game, usually followed on Boxing Day by the return match, was something we accepted as the norm. Boxing Day was 'get your own back day' as there were one or two debts to be repaid from the day before. Come Easter, there was always the Good Friday game, the Easter Saturday match the day after, then the Easter Monday game—three games in four days! Cup replays added vital games mid week but we just soldiered on and rubbed our hands on the following Thursday. This was when we drew two pay packets and two more the following week when another game was chalked up on the Saturday giving us four games in nine days. It was hectic but financially rewarding. Well, it was rewarding when winning that is, especially in cup ties or crucial games for league positions but when losing, the few quid in the packet sometimes made you wonder what the hell you were doing there.

Winning pay gave the average player two wages in the week including his pay from work (don't forget that the vast majority of players held down a weekday job away from football). To a young, married man or a single Jack the Lad, two pay packets helped considerably to lead a decent lifestyle. The dressing room banter stopped when the chairman came in, just before the players went out onto the field, to tell them what the winning bonus was and, usually, a satisfied smile would appear on the faces of the players. This method of announcing bonuses was used at Leeds. Other clubs had their own way of announcing bonuses on the day. I have worked with chairmen who told me the bonus and I passed it on to the players. Each club also had a different pay scale. In my time at Leeds the players signed on each year to play for a minimum winning pay of £30 and losing pay would be set at £15. The players knew that they would never simply get the £30 when they won because the minimum payment carried a bonus for winning which the Chairman told them about before each game. It may not be the same amount from one week to the other but it was rarely below the steady £200 bonus for league games, rising to a maximum of around £300 for vital fixtures. Cup ties were better for the players as the further the team went in the various cups then the more money they received. Winning the Challenge Cup in those days could pull anything from £1,000 to £1,500 per man and that was just for the final. A good bonus was paid out in all the rounds of the Challenge Cup after a win.

Most clubs put on some sort of food for the players after training such as soup, a sandwich or beans on toast. This was because some players had come straight from work to train. The food after the match varied among clubs and some clubs, usually traditional ones, put on a real north country man's spread. One club, Whitehaven, put on a superb meat pie and chips, Batley's masterpiece was apple pie and thick, delicious sandwiches whilst the clubs who possessed their own kitchen provided a sit down meal. Leeds did a nice chicken with vegetables and Bradford, Saints, Wigan, Hull FC and Hull Kingston Rovers provided a similar meal.

So those mud covered, freezing cold days gave way to the sunny, laid back, spotlessly clean days of summer football. One might think this is far more civilised than it used to be. I suppose so, but the old winter game had something that somehow rose above the adverse playing conditions. It had something magical that lifted one's spirits when attending a game. Of course not all games were played on glue-pot pitches. There were plenty of firm grounds, especially when frosty. But most of the grounds in winter were, in racing parlance, good to soft. There was a saying in those days that mud brought everybody down to the same pace. Well the likes of Brian Bevan, Billy Boston, Jim Lewthwaite, Andrew Turnbull and Lionel Cooper must have found the only dry areas on all fields. In all this mud, snow and rain, these men would run in 40 tries before Christmas. They and players like Dicky Williams, Willie Horne, Willie Davies, Cec Mountford, Alex Murphy, Lewis Jones, Dave Bolton, Neil Fox, Eric Ashton, Mick Sullivan and Alan Davies were the 'magic' of the game. Their magic made one forget the clinging mud and the biting wind. Are the fundamental differences seen today between winter and summer rugby league games purely down to the climate change between now and the old winter sport? Or is it down to something so simple that we could miss it? Could it be that all the changes made to our game from the winter game to now are responsible for the players not being as good as they were then? We have a great game, we also had a great winter game. Let's somehow maintain our traditions of 100 winters.

10

ONE AND TWO DIVISION SYSTEM

Our league division system has changed many times since the breakaway. The first fixtures played in the Northern Union featured 22 clubs of which 15 are still active in professional rugby league and eight of those 15 still operate in Super League at the time of writing. These teams are Huddersfield, Wakefield, St Helens, Warrington, Bradford ,Wigan, Leeds and Hull FC. At the time of the first Annual General Meeting, Mr H.H. Waller announced that there were now 59 clubs in membership. Because of the growth of interested clubs the new Union decided to form a Yorkshire Senior Competition and a Lancashire Senior Competition. In the 1895–96 season, 22 clubs formed the Northern Union League with 11 teams each in the two Senior competitions. Two further leagues were formed, the Yorkshire and Lancashire 'seconds' to accommodate new clubs wanting to be members. By 1901 the top clubs in the Northern Union League were whispering together about forming a 'super' league. Twelve clubs met at Huddersfield and voted to submit a resolution that 12 clubs should compete in a Northern League.

The pressure grew on the 12 to increase the number and an additional two clubs were admitted. The cry was 'closed shop' and accusations were fired at the lucky 14, who were Leigh, Runcorn, Hull FC, Huddersfield, Batley, Halifax, Swinton, Brighouse

Rangers, Hunslet, Bradford, Warrington, Broughton Rangers, Oldham, Salford. To alleviate these accusations, it was decided that the bottom team would drop into either of the senior competitions depending on their county and a play off for promotion would take place between the two leaders of the county leagues. Tired of the political infighting to gain a place in the 'big' league, Hull Kingston Rovers made a protest by joining the Lancashire Senior Competition. Those left out in Lancashire formed the South-West Lancashire league and the South-East Lancashire league and these two leagues agreed to play fixtures against the Northern League.

The Yorkshire Senior Competition organised a new league when they invited the Yorkshire 'seconds' to form a new league with the teams not wanted in the Northern League. The 'new look' Yorkshire Senior Competition now had a 14 team league and included some recognisable names and some strange ones, Leeds, Castleford, Wakefield Trinity, Dewsbury, Keighley, Bramley, York, Manningham, Goole, Heckmondwike, Normanton, Sowerby Bridge, Liversedge and Holbeck. The two new Lancashire leagues had made an agreement with the Northern League about the signing of their players but made no agreement with the new Yorkshire Senior Competition and there were some strained meetings during the 1901–02 season as Yorkshire players were signed into the bigger league. In the summer of 1902, two divisions of the Northern League with 18 teams in the first and 12 in the second were formed. Later this was amended to 18 in each division. Wigan, St Helens, Hull Kingston Rovers and Widnes were admitted into the first division. The winners of the Yorkshire Senior Competition, Leeds, were surprisingly omitted and they joined another 17 clubs in division two. In 1903–04 Wakefield Trinity finished top of the second division and were promoted. In second place St Helens and Holbeck played off for the other promotion spot. Saints won and Holbeck Rugby Club turned from rugby to soccer, changing their name to Leeds City and a few years later became Leeds United.

Because of the 'death' of so many second division clubs, the 1905 general meeting decided to merge both divisions into one and end the two division system. The 'new' league caused problems as it consisted of 31 teams. The problem was resolved as 31 teams would play 60 games. Clubs were asked to compile their own fixtures featuring 'derby' matches and playing as many of last season's first division versus first division teams as possible. The idea of playing 60 games per club in one season was out of the question. The thorn in the side of every secretary was removed once and for all with the final abolition of the 'working rule' so that a player no longer had to prove he was in work before he could play on Saturdays. There was further disruption when second division teams withdrew from the league and Cheshire, Durham and Northumberland resigned from the union. This left only three counties to fight out the county championship, Lancashire, Cumberland and Yorkshire. The 1905–06 season saw Leigh declared League Champions on a percentage basis with Hunslet in second place. The number of clubs in the league meant that not all clubs played each other home and away. Hunslet made a strong point that Leigh had, because of the fixture set up, played an 'easy' season as they had hardly played any of the tough Yorkshire sides and had been 'given' the championship. This bust up caused a meeting to be held and the fixture format for 1906–07 season thrashed out. This included a 'play off' at the season's end by the top four clubs in the league with the two winners going into the Championship final, to be played on a neutral ground. In the first one Halifax defeated Oldham 18–3 at Huddersfield before a crowd of 13,200.

The First World War ended the competition from the 1914–15 season when Huddersfield beat Leeds in the final 35–2 at Wakefield's Belle Vue before a crowd of 14,000. The competition restarted in 1919–20 when Hull FC won the title by beating Huddersfield 3–2 at Headingley in front of 12,900 spectators. The one-league system continued for 20 unbroken years until the outbreak of the Second World War when the rugby league supplied thousands of men to the war effort and the game continued with the war time league in which any available player from any club not playing could be registered as a 'guest'. The end of season Championships were named 'War Time Emergency Play Offs of the War League' and for the first two seasons the Yorkshire and Lancashire League Champions met in a two leg final. Bradford Northern were the dominant team and won the first one in 1939–40 by beating Swinton by an aggregate score of 37–22. The second year, Bradford beat Wigan on aggregate 45–15. The following season, 1941–42, a one off final was played at Headingley when Dewsbury, under the astute management of Eddie Waring, beat Bradford at Headingley by 13–0. Back to the two legs in 1942–43 when Dewsbury beat Halifax 11–3 at Crown Flatt and 22–13 at Thrum Hall. This championship was declared null and void as Dewsbury were proved to have played an ineligible player. In 1943–44 Wigan beat Dewsbury 25–14 on aggregate and in 1944–45 Bradford beat Halifax on a 26–20 aggregate.

At the end of the war, the one league competition continued amid traditional clubs leaving and new clubs arriving. Life went on in its usual way until the two divisions were reintroduced in the 1962–63 season. This lasted only two seasons and reverted to one league until a definite period of two divisional football was embraced again in the 1973–74 season. A system of four teams up, four teams down operated from the start until 1985–86 when three teams, Leigh, Barrow and Wakefield Trinity were promoted and York, Swinton and Dewsbury came down. The 1986–87 season saw four clubs relegated again, Oldham, Featherstone Rovers, Barrow and Wakefield Trinity and two clubs, Hunslet and Swinton promoted.

From then on, promotion and relegation continued at three up, three down until a Third Division was introduced in 1990–91. This division was introduced to allow teams who had struggled against the high scoring 'big guns', to build up their playing strength and gain promotion into the now eight team second division. This idea, called the 'Hetherington Plan', the brainchild of the then Sheffield Eagles Chairman, Gary Hetherington, lasted only one season, then the divisions reverted back to two until the formation of Super League.

The ups and downs, the changes and alterations and the fluctuations of various clubs' fortunes, began on day one of rugby league and still continue. Something was always being altered for the good. On the field, scrimmaging was a problem, then we had years of discontent with the play the ball. We changed the kick off rule for a short while with the team just scoring, kicking the ball back to the opposition. We even changed the field set up from three lines across the field, two '25' lines and a half way line to a line at every 10 meters. We took scrums from 5 yards to 10 yards then to 20 metres from the touchline, and worst of all, we took the competition from the scrimmage. We even changed the points value for tries and drop goals. We changed the rules to stop accurate kicking of the ball, then we brought in a rule to reward a good kick and we moved our beloved game to the summer. Virtually overnight the game totally changed to suit television. The league system was abolished to cater for a 'closed shop' type of league where a good ground was considered paramount above tradition. I suppose in some respects we have moved on for the better, but I consider we have lost an immense amount of glorious tradition which is disgracefully ignored by the modern game and its media. This tradition will never be recovered.

11

YOUTH POLICIES AND DISCIPLINE

Almost every club, since the Second World War, conducted a youth policy. This was not a policy devoted to develop youth from junior teams run from the club but from signing promising youngsters from the junior amateur game. Each club had a 'chief scout', usually a former player, whose job it was to scour the junior leagues and make a list of youngsters whom he considered a good enough prospect to sign. The chief scout headed a team of experienced men who would cover as many games as possible at weekends, some checking on players for a second opinion, some looking at youngsters for the first time and in some cases asking the player to tell his parents to contact the club to meet the club's directors. Some youngsters were asked to play trial games, usually three, but adult players were also sought from the amateur ranks. These players were considered good first team material.

Different geographical areas produced varying numbers of players. For instance the Yorkshire area relied on the Featherstone, Castleford and Wakefield towns and the villages around them. Mining districts always produced plenty of good amateur players. Possibly the most famous of all, Sharlston, introduced the 'endless belt' system and over the years turned out hundreds of excellent professional players, including international players. Our game was and, to a certain extent, still is a parochial game. Fathers played, so sons played and a long family involvement could be traced back to grandads and sometimes great grandads. Also the districts in which one lived had a huge bearing on which game one played and of course, which team one supported. Nowadays one is inclined to associate soccer supporters with fervent following of teams but I have known a number of rugby league men who would not go to a certain ground, so much did they dislike the team that played there. A classic case of this was caused by the intense rivalry between the Leeds and Hunslet clubs. Two regular and staunch Leeds supporters who lived in our street would not go to Parkside, even to support Leeds!

The biggest influence on one's rugby league career, as either player or supporter, was the school one attended. Luckily for me, our school, The Sacred Heart RC, was a rugby school. We played our first game in September 1945 against Broad Lane C of E. In the second division where we played there were 10 teams. In the first division were the big guns, the schools with three times the number of kids attending compared to Sacred Heart. In Leeds there were 14 teams in the division and a total of 24 schools playing rugby league, some with two teams. Hunslet schools had as many so there was always plenty of scope for the three City of Leeds professional teams to look for talent. Team scouts were present at all inter town and city representative games where teams from all over the county played for the City Championship. I remember playing as a 15 year old against York, Hunslet, Hull, Castleford, Featherstone and Wakefield schools. The winners of the Yorkshire area then played in a three leg play off against Lancashire and Cumberland schools. County rugby league teams were selected from the inter town and city games and the main game was the Lancashire versus Yorkshire clash. In the late 1940s and early 1950s there were no age restricted rugby leagues for 15 year olds to play in. The lowest age group was under 18 and to give three years away at 15 was asking too much, even for the keenest of youngsters. I remember I was 'roped in' to play for a lovely little club, Burley Vale and I found the age difference to be a huge barrier. Whilst I gave a good account of myself, week after week confrontations of competing against bigger, stronger, faster and much older players was, to say the least, unfair to me and the other 15 year olds pulled into the side. But that is how one learned the game then.

The age difference when playing at school somehow never bothered us. When I started playing for the school I was nine years old. I played against 14 year olds, as there were no age restrictions. Not one youngster bothered about this but as we reached 15 years old and played against, in some cases, almost 19 year olds the physical difference told. Suddenly, the year I left school in 1951, a Junior League was formed within the Leeds and District League and an advert in the *Yorkshire Evening Post* told of a newly formed team asking for 15 year old school leavers who wanted to play rugby league for Leeds junior side to turn up at Headingley for training. A few of us did this and that took care of football in my own age group. The other two professional clubs did the same and played as Hunslet Supporters and Bramley Supporters. We played as Headingley Juniors. The Leeds and District stretched across the county a wee bit and encompassed Dewsbury and Batley.

All around us new leagues started, the Bradford League, York League, Wakefield League and Castleford and Featherstone League. In Lancashire, professional clubs took youngsters under their wing and started teams funded by the senior club. The official youth policies began, although the players were still at amateur level until they were 17. Then, if the player was good enough, they were signed. Older players in open age amateur rugby league continued to be signed but the under 17 year old and under 19 year old leagues were the forerunner to the later 'Colts' leagues which included signed on youngsters. From the Colts came the Academy teams in which players could be fully signed on professionals from an early age.

The progression of a young player was simple. He went, gradually, from the restricted age level teams through to the 'A' team. This was a club's 'second' team, a vehicle used to bring players back to fitness from injury, to play a trialist in, to have a look at youngsters to see how they shaped and to play their young signings in, giving them chance to develop against some decent players before making the big step into first team football. Used correctly, the 'A' team was worth every penny, used for the wrong reasons it could be a millstone around the club's neck. The 'A' teams played in two leagues, the Eastern County teams played in the Yorkshire Senior Competition, a throwback name to the late 1890s, and the Western teams played in the Lancashire Combination. There was a cup and a shield to play for in the 'A' team leagues. The Yorkshire Senior Competition played for a superb, large, ornate silver cup. The Lancastrians played for a superb silver shield, another wonderful trophy. The youngsters playing in this league could be up against former or even current internationals. There would be possibly county players in the league and certainly lots of well known former first team players, all there for a youngster to try out his ability against. There lies the reason for the massive change in the league set up. The clubs against the 'A' teams wanted them removed because of the cost of running them. The major complaint was that too many old stagers were 'pinching' money in the 'A' team. Something had to be put back in its place because of the important job the old 'A' team did. The under 21 year old sides that most of the progressive clubs run now have filled the gap left when 'A' teams were removed. Each team can have a restricted number of over 21 players. This covers the injury, trialist and development problem that the pro 'A' team brigade feared had been lost.

There was never anything in place to deal with further education as there is today. A young player had a full time job and that was considered enough to teach the youngster the vital disciplines of life in the big world once they had left school. The workplace was also a place of learning as were the training nights and playing afternoons. The young player, just signed for a professional club would have several mentors, his parents, his boss at work and his coach at his football club. This possibly explains why not many young players were up in court. The cross section of players in the rugby league and the work they did varied. The majority had manual jobs but there were plenty of school teachers and office workers. Of the manual workers, there were many National Coal Board employees. Colliers from around the Yorkshire and Lancashire coalfields and from the deep and dangerous under sea pits up in Cumberland around Whitehaven and Workington made up the many teams from these areas. There was an old saying in Yorkshire that if you wanted a forward, go to the top of any shaft in Castleford and Featherstone, shout down for one and hundreds would answer the call. There were fire fighters, police officers, joiners, brickies, plasterers, labourers, bus drivers, mill workers, brewers, salesmen, bank clerks, coal haulers, pub landlords, welders, electricians, tilers, tailors, in fact every single job imaginable was represented in the professional ranks of the Rugby Football League.

Most players lived within easy travelling distance of his club but some did travel to training. When I coached at Workington, David Ward the former Great Britain and Leeds hooker and I would travel up to Cumbria twice a week to train and again on Sundays for home matches. We would pick up another two players, who lived in Lancashire, at the Preston turn off on the M6 and off we would go up to the far north west. The youth policies of clubs before the Colts era were based on simple logic. If a club signed 10 youngsters and only one of that 10 'made it', then the policy had been a success. Clubs had a set fee for signing youngsters and it was not exorbitant. If a youngster made the grade then he became a sellable article on the transfer market. The buying and selling of players in those days did not only create interest amongst the clubs' supporters, it maintained a healthy cash flow throughout the game.

While the game of rugby league was often more brutal than it is today, where players were adjudged to have transgressed the rules then discipline was often harsh. Should the referee dismiss a player from the field of play, the official submitted a report, giving the most minute details of the dismissal, to the Rugby Football League HQ and the player would be notified of the disciplinary committee's decision of their findings. The player could make a personal appearance but charged a fee that would be forfeited if the player was found guilty. The decisions were few and short—Guilty, Not guilty, Sending off sufficient, Mistaken identity or No case to answer. The disciplinary committee informed the club secretary about any given suspension first and passed an enclosed letter to the player confirming the suspension. The player could appeal but a fee was involved, with no return of fee if the appeal failed. Not many players appealed unless the suspension was a major one. There was little compassion in the suspensions handed out. The Disciplinary Committee considered nothing except the actions within the context of the offence. Appearing on appeal brought many humorous moments for the committee as some of the excuses were hilarious. One well known, tough forward sent off for a late tackle on an opponent accepted that the tackle was late but his defence was that he had arrived at the tackle as early as he could! The player lost his appeal and his fee!

When a player was waiting to be admitted into the committee's presence in the Council Chamber at RLHQ, they waited in an anteroom until called for. One player waited quite a long time and the committee's sandwiches and flask of tea were brought into the anteroom for their break between cases. The player waited so long that he decided to have a sandwich or two and ended up eating the lot. When brought before the committee he was found Not guilty of the match offence but given a three match ban for eating the sandwiches. About the worst offence a player could be up for was striking, lifting a hand against or man handling the referee or touch judge. One or two players have, in the history of the game, man handled the official and on being found guilty have been suspended Sine Die, as stated in the dictionary, with no appointed date for resumption. This could mean suspension for life, although sometimes the suspension would be lifted after a few years. The last life suspension I can remember was Gwyn Davies who played for Dewsbury. He was accused and found guilty of deliberately running into the referee, Mr R.L. Thomas [Oldham], during a game at Crown Flatt. He was suspended for a long time, finally released from suspension to retire soon after.

Some hilarious tales emerged from the disciplinary committee room. I knew of a player who, through a sheer accident, stood on the chairman of the disciplinary committee's dog's paw. A few weeks later he was up before the committee who gave him a four game suspension and the chairman added on two games for standing on his dog! For many years a player who had been sent off had little or no representation at his hearing. The committee simply looked at his past record, examined a written report of the incident from the referee and that was that. One could arrange a 'personal appearance' but that could be a lot worse than accepting the committee's judgement. Most players accepted their suspensions and did their time. The referee's word was law and he was not required to attend a personal appearance, his report was enough. The player was rarely found 'not guilty'.

12

COACHES, TRAINING AND TACTICS

Look up the definition of the word 'coach' and different dictionaries will give slightly varying definitions. These will be 'instructor', 'tutor', 'trainer in sport' and one I particularly subscribe to, 'the corrector of mistakes'. I also think that 'team organiser' is another term that a decent coach would accept as a description of his work. The modern day coach, at almost every club, has a large team of assistants to help him prepare his side for the weekly assault on their strength and fitness. In the old days, it may astound the young folk and newcomers to the game to know that the average number of staff who coached, conditioned and prepared the two teams from the club was two. These two men, coach and assistant coach, acted not only as coaches but also in a succession of jobs: statistics taker, conditioner, coach, father figure, parish priest, short term money lender, strong disciplinarian and above all a fountain of truth to all players.

Nowadays the physiotherapist is a vital cog in the staff armoury. These days there seems to be a surfeit of qualified physios but that was not always the case. Only the big clubs had the type of physio we accept today. At some clubs he would be a former player who took several first aid courses at work. He would be a sensible, honest sort of a bloke who, if in any doubt, would send the player to hospital. I served as coach to the Halifax club and because of the shortage of both money and qualified practitioners, had to act as physio for half a season or so.

Coaches were nowhere to be seen for many years in our game. The first coach to be taken on a Lions tour was as late as 1958 when the first Great Britain coach to take a touring side was Jim Brough the former Leeds and Great Britain full back. Two tours were sent out after that, in 1962 and 1966, without a coach. The practice resumed in 1970 when Johnny Whiteley the former Hull FC and Great Britain loose forward took the last successful ashes winning Great Britain team to Australia and New Zealand. When on tour without a coach, the captain of the side took on the mantel. Possibly the first coach to gain fame was the great Welshman, Dai Rees of Halifax then Bradford Northern. Another great Welshman, Jim Sullivan, did wonderfully well at Wigan and St Helens just after the Second World War. The great Ces Mountford, Wigan's post war brilliant Kiwi stand off half, moved into coaching at Warrington with tremendous success and before him, Frank 'Dolly' Dawson, a tough Hunslet forward had successful spells at Leeds then Halifax. Joe Egan, Wigan's great hooker coached for a long time and was respected throughout the league.

The term coach changes the whole idea of an experienced man being in charge of team matters. Before the term coach was used, all clubs had a trainer. In the old team pictures he would be the man, usually in his shirt sleeves, with a towel over his arm. Just how much input into the workings of the team the trainer had varied from club to club but no trainer ever had the overall power of total team selection. That was the prerogative of the board of directors. They selected both the teams, the first team and the 'A' team and simply gave the trainer a sheet of paper with the selections on it. He notified the team and it was the trainer's responsibility to ensure that this team won. There is such a huge difference in the running of the team today. Then the trainer, who in reality was the coach, had to devise the team's tactics and his job was on the line if the players the board selected did not shape up.

The end of the Second World War saw changes in the running of teams in the professional game. Gradually the old selection committees were replaced by the coach who, it was realised, was employed to bring success to his club. He should have the say as to which players played and, at many clubs, which players were bought and sold. This issue, of the coach buying and selling players, was one jealously held onto by some clubs' boards of directors. It was established that the job of coach would have to include these issues if success was expected. Part of the requirements of a coach was that he knew the game and its players inside out. This huge change did not happen overnight. The board of directors' way of hanging on to the basic signings of players was to introduce a 'football director'. This board member worked closely with the coach to identify players needed by the club and take the coach's comments on these players back to the boardroom. Usually the football director did any financial negotiating with the selling club but mostly the coach talked to the player to find out how much he wanted from the deal. The coach reported his findings to the football director. If the player wanted too much money and would not negotiate, then the deal would be off. In most cases the coach and player sorted out their differences.

Coaches were just ordinary blokes with the same frailties and weaknesses as anybody else. Young players in particular sometimes felt a wee bit afraid of the coach. On the training paddock the coach wore his serious fault finding face. In the dressing room he was more relaxed and would laugh and joke with the players. The most serious time for the coach was match day, when everything had to be correct. The timing of his team hitting maximum impetus was imperative, coming to the boil too soon meant that this crucial impetus may be left in the dressing room and the team's performance would be marred.

In the original days of the Northern Union, the captain and the trainer mainly looked to the running of the team. The tactics in those tough, early days were dictated by the size and power of one's pack of forwards. These hard, durable men made ground and took play into a position from which the three quarters came into the game. The half back fetched and carried acting as kind of link between the stand off half and the forwards. Once in possession, the stand off half would attempt to create a gap somewhere in the opposition defensive line for his centres to hit. Then the wingmen came into play. This simple style of play ensured that the wingmen had ample room and enough possession to score many glorious and crowd pleasing tries. One must remember that the forwards in those days were not chosen for pace, that job belonged to the three quarters. The forwards were the 'labourers' and the three quarters the 'craftsmen'. The packs would graft, unceasingly, all through the game. They won the ball from the scrum when only brave men would approach that melee, as it was a hard place to be. They won the ball from the then line-outs, which were not as evenly structured as in today's rugby union games, and again the term 'anything goes' applied. They won the ball from the terrible rucks and brutal mauls that ensued at almost every dropped ball. They forced themselves up field in a series of strength sapping charges and drives to make field positions from which lightening quick backs were unleashed upon the opposition. This was the point of the introduction of the half back. After a strong charge, he would get his partner, the stand off, stepping away to find a path for his centres. The teams practised this sort of play under the guidance of the captain and the trainer time after time, except of course for when they were not running.

The trainer at all clubs maintained a type of training that was handed down from trainer to trainer: run, run, run. The alternative to running was skipping! Like boxers in training, skipping built up stamina, good foot action and strong arms. Whichever club one went to there was always a pile of skipping ropes. The area for training, weather permitting, was the rugby pitch. In times of heavy rain, road running or working out in the club's grandstand, up and down the terraces, was the order of the day. Road running entailed miles of hard slog, up gradients and freewheeling down the slopes, a stop at a given point where a series of exercises were completed painstakingly, then a long, good pace back to the ground for some skipping.

Clubs with a good financial backing used other amenities at which to train. Some local swimming baths had a sprung floor cover over the pool and this was one type of indoor training facility that could be used. Of course there were no sports or leisure centres then and it took all the trainer's ingenuity to come up with training venues in the depths of winter. There were no weight training facilities as such anywhere. Weights were not considered an asset to training for rugby league and, when first signing as a professional in 1953, as I discussed earlier, I distinctly remember the coach, a well known and well respected man, strongly advising me against doing three exercises that would be detrimental to playing rugby. These exercises were swimming, weight training and cycling, 'These things develop muscles that will obstruct your running ability', said the coach.

Our game was stuck in the 'dark ages' for years and it took the schoolmasters of PE to break the barrier of ignorance regarding physical fitness. As the PE teachers gradually entered the game as players, they brought with them a new science, that of modern conditioning to achieve a high level of excellence in fitness. A little later came the fitness revolution with the opening of the already mentioned sports centres with their state of the art gyms. Hardly any rugby league club had the semblance of a gym and I suppose there was a good reason to the way of thinking then. Most players had heavy manual jobs. The weight training was done at work, down the mine or on the building site, in the steel yards or in the foundry. In the work place almost everything was lifted, pushed or pulled. The most up to date technology in equipment was the shovel! A hard day's work meant just that and the need for bulging muscles was not an issue, they bulged enough from hard graft at work. A former Australian Test player once told me that he was absolutely sure that he knew the exact time of the demise of Great Britain as a Test match force in rugby league. He said that it was the day that they introduced total machinery into the mines. In other words the problem was the automation of the work place.

Every player dreaded the fitness work done in the grandstand terraces. The continuous boredom of hitting one step after the other and the strain on the legs was both mind boggling and downright dangerous. From the base line at ground level, one jogged up to the back of the stand wall and down again, time after time. Sometimes as a variation, one would have to carry a team mate in fireman's lift fashion up the terrace, then in piggy back fashion. Thankfully, players never carried anyone down the terrace as it was considered too dangerous! Occasionally, as a complete change which made one's legs ache for a week, was walking backwards up the terrace.

Bricklayer's labourers did this type of exercise easily as they spent all day walking up and down ladders carrying a hod full of bricks. A few clubs had areas under the stand where a sprint track was laid. Sprinting in training was considered a paramount necessity. Usually the track would be made of fine cinders, which when rolled flat was as good as any surface on which to sprint. Trainers who knew their trade would badger the posh club directors to buy each player a pair of running spikes. These shoes, of course, taught one to run on one's toes rather than flat footed. Forwards as well as backs were expected to sprint train. In the early days of the Northern Union forwards training was done to induce strength, stamina and power. Pace, at the breakaway in 1895, was the domain of the backs, the fleet footed smaller men and to ask a forward to sprint train in those days was not done for fear of physical attack. The forward's main type of training was lapping the field making sure that they rounded the touchline at the corner flags. They would jog around in small groups talking about facets of the game unheard of by three quarters. How to wheel the scrum, how to block the opposition hooker from getting near the ball as it was put into the scrum and generally how to make the scrum as uncomfortable as possible for the other team's front row. The practice of scrimmaging was done with a mixture of first team and 'A' team forwards. Sometimes for a bit of fun the trainer would call the three quarters over to form a pack against the first team scrum. 'Just to let you know what it's like in there,' the trainer would tell the backs. I can assure the reader that they didn't like it at all. Again one must remember that it was a competitive scrum then unlike today's huddle.

The coach of those days was a very different animal to coaches today. Some simply maintained the clothes they had travelled to the ground in and put on a pair of football socks and football boots, tucked their trousers into the socks and went out onto the training paddock in their raincoat or heavy overcoat. The principle of 'Do as I say and not as I do', was adhered to but they, overall, were fine men, usually with a brand of humour that somehow went with their lofty position. They were men who possessed a strong personality, men who were idolised in some cases by the players but above all they were men trusted by the club and all associated with it.

Most coaches were tactically sound, having had vast experience in the game as players. Some were former players who had become students in the arts of rugby league football. For some reason these men were called 'thinking coaches'. Suddenly these 'students' began to introduce new ideas and concepts into fitness training and game tactics. Defence, for so long an almost untouched area, was studied and brought into the modern game as a tactic and not something that just 'had to be done'. Don't get me wrong, there were some fantastic tacklers in the old game and British coaches in the 1980s attempted to come to grips with some issues. They considered the problems of sliding defences, of left and right sided players, of the double marker system working hard and not going into that position to rest, of the old stagers 'covering the blind side' and hiding away from the hard work of tackling. But the emphasis on organised, constructive and destructive team defence came into fruition only after the introduction of Super League.

The 1982 'Invincibles', the superb, touring Australians introduced a myriad of new innovations in their play that left us dumbfounded. They were organised in every department of the game. They introduced mental preparation for a game, the tactical use of tackle shields—a wonderful new idea—free standing tackle bags, which had been around in rugby union in Britain for years but we never noticed them, rolling tractor tyres for practising one's technique in the actual physical tackle. In fact they brought the message of a new and fresh outlook to an old, tired game. Those Invincibles dictated, in 1982, how our beloved game should be played and also showed us just how far behind we were in perception, preparation, practice techniques, fitness and the area in which we always insisted we were advanced, the skills of the game. They blew us away and left us in a state of shock. They made us realise that their team were three divisions above us and worst of all they inflicted such a traumatic lesson upon us that we have never quite recovered to this day. Most thinking coaches in this country looked on and were dazzled by the Australians' success, not only by the results on that tour (the Aussies went unbeaten) but on how they played the game. Their kicking game brought a new dimension, their passing almost mesmerised us and their strength and pace were unbelievable.

That was only the beginning as subsequent home and away tours proved that there was no letting up. We have improved a little since then and no doubt, because of full time professionalism, we will get better but the huge advantage, gained by the 1982 tourists, not only constructed a physical wall between us but an even bigger psychological wall. The coach, over the 100 year's evolvement of our game, regularly had to adjust his thinking and tactics to suit the various law changes that occurred. In the old days the trainers had to live through the traumas of two players being dropped from the team when the team shrank from 15 to 13 players. They saw the line-out abolished and watched the old game gradually change into something like the game played today. Later coaches had to come to grips with other changes to the game. These changes included unchallenged scrums, an extra five metres on the off side rule at the play the ball, not being able to steal the ball in the tackle if assisted by a team mate and an increase in points for a try and winning a point in the league even if beaten [may the Good Lord preserve us].

The coach kept a kind of dossier on opposition players. The players that the coach considered to be poor catchers of high balls were peppered with high kicks. All coaches subscribed to the idea of running their big, strong forwards into the scrum half and stand off of the opposition. The coach targeted the weaker defenders and sent in his 'heavy armour' against them. He would also investigate the weather conditions on the day of the game and advise his charges of the type of attacks likely to be made by the opposition. There was always the type of good player the coach pointed out for rougher treatment, usually the ball handler or key attacker. Many coaches used the old adage of 'Stop so and so and you stop their team'.

Some coaches would be more specific, 'Give him one early on and he'll surrender'. The most misused statement by some coaches was, 'Give it to him early because he doesn't like it'. My reaction to that was to think, 'Who does?' Nobody likes being smashed in the face with an elbow or a full-blooded punch or being dropped upon from a great height with someone's knees in the kidneys. Nor does anyone like being kicked in the unmentionables, but the coach's advice implied that type of treatment. The truth was that it was hard to 'catch' a good player except when they were getting older and a wee bit slower! The anecdote that the good footballer used to protect himself was handed down from the senior players who always advised leading into the tackler, 'With your elbow covering your jaw', or in other words, give it to him before he gives it to you! Three of the better footballers I knew all suffered serious jaw injuries in their latter years, John Holmes [Leeds], Roger Millward [Hull Kingston Rovers] and the best uncapped utility player I ever worked with, Johnny Woolford [Bramley, Bradford Northern and Dewsbury]. All three players were superb ball handlers but there were many more who 'got caught'.

Most coaches employed a similar game plan in different areas of the field. Carrying the ball out of one's danger area, one's own quarter of the field, the coach expected a set of 'safety first' plays, the dummy half running directly from the base of the ruck of the play the ball or one pass to a safe handling forward, what the Kiwi's call 'first cab off the rank'. This forward would make as much ground as possible, then, on the final play, a kick, which in the old days we called a 'downtown', a well directed long kick down field. In the midfield area the coach expected a slight increase in flair as his half backs came more into play and worked in ball work practice on various set moves from the play the ball. A simple set piece would be, on gaining possession, to hit the ball towards a touchline in the first two drives, then ping the ball quickly across field. If tackled, continue to hit the ball the same way around, then on the forth tackle spin the ball back towards the start of the move and if there was no success, then hit a high kick to the posts or a grubber into the opponent's in goal area. This was a simple move but, in its day, very effective.

Inside the opponent's quarter, the tactics changed again as the coach would have worked on several close in moves, mostly designed around one of two decoy runners. These short play moves were the domain of the big, strong runners and the clever half back. The thinking coach had plans for most situations and were well known for their crafty tactics. Unlike today, another area of craft was the tap penalty. Players spent hundreds of hours during the season practising various set piece plays from the tap penalty. Alas today that style of attack has lost its appeal to the modern coach and we see half backs and three quarters taking the ball up from these dead ball situations. This used to be the forward's area and no backs were allowed in there.

Moves from the scrum were also worked on with regularity and the then 10 metre 'blind side' was used many times by the ultra skilful scrum half and loose forward combination. Each club had a trio of players, named the 'eternal triangle', the stand off half, scrum half and loose forward, whose understanding and reading of each other's play seemed to be almost supernatural. Their combinations of plays brought an added excitement and another dimension to their team's attack. The loose forward's masterly control of the blind side of the scrum and the danger area around that set piece was always a talking point at games. All loose forwards possessed these skills. Speaking of that crucial position, his official number was 13. Now, as we know, 13 is an unlucky number so some clubs in the old days had number 14 instead of 13. Now, of course, because of squad numbering, any number can be found playing anywhere on the field and, again, to cover the blind side, a loose forward was allowed to stand out of the pack to defend that vital channel on the short side.

All that changed when the loose forward attached himself to

every scrum. Many old ideas passed down through the years from trainer to trainer and coach to coach and most coaches travelled every avenue to win games. Some coaches advised against rolling one's sleeves up, as forwards were inclined to do, in wet weather. The rain or snow on a player's arms may well act as a 'bar of soap', as we used to say, and the sleeves rolled down gave extra protection against dropping the ball. Players rubbed powdered resin into their hands before leaving the dressing room. This added an extra rough, dry surface to one's hands and helped to hold and control the ball.

But all in all, the coach introduced varied tactics against different clubs and foul play was never an issue. Obviously the game itself demanded that one should be able to look after one's self because of the physical contact required to play it. The degree of force used was totally down to the individual player and whilst most players developed a 'hard' nature, not all developed a 'dirty' nature. Therefore even in the fiercest battles, very little went above the 'hard' level. Those who ventured across the acceptable line were known by the players and above all by the referees. Nevertheless, some older, more experienced players had many tricks to allow them an advantage. In those days on winning the toss one could choose either to kick off or at which end of the field to defend. Some believed fervently that if they won the toss, they should always kick off, giving the opposition the ball and in the days of unlimited tackles, knocking the hell out of the opposition with fierce early tackling. This was known as the 'softening up' treatment. Many coaches also believed in this system.

So, from the tough, knock 'em over, forward orientated coach to the run, run, run coach who thought only of sweeping passing from one side of the field to the other, the full spectrum of coaching styles were many and varied. Huddersfield, Leeds, Wigan, Salford, Saints, Hull Kingston Rovers and Workington Town were renowned for their speedy play with three quarters to the fore. Widnes, Wakefield

Trinity, Leigh, Belle Vue Rangers, Bradford Northern, Hull, Halifax and Barrow would rely on a big pack of forwards to create openings for their speed men. The styles were different and the tactics were never the same for any team, none were tailored the same.

13

INTERNATIONALS
AND TOURS

To be selected for a British Lions tour of Australia and New Zealand was the highest honour one could achieve. Usually two players from each position were picked meaning 26 players were chosen to tour. Our first tour of the antipodes occurred in 1910 and tourists left in two parties. The second party included players involved in the Cup and Championship finals. The first party arrived at the end of May and the second arrived on 2 June after a long sail. The outward ports of call were Gibraltar, Marseilles, Malta, Port Said, Aden, Bombay, Colombo, Fremantle, Adelaide, Melbourne and Sydney. Some trip! Homeward bound the team left Sydney to Auckland across to Taranaki then had the long haul up through the Panama Canal at Colon, then to Curacao and finally across the Atlantic to London. Travelling to and from Australia took almost eight weeks each way.

On the first tour, only two Tests were played in Australia, one each in Sydney and Brisbane, and one in Auckland. The team played 18 games in all with a tourists' record of played 18, won 13, drawn 1 lost 4. As already mentioned in *Chapter 1* and *Chapter 3*, the Australians toured Britain in 1908–09 and A.H. Baskerville's 'All Gold's', a mixture of Australian and mostly Kiwi players, toured in 1907–08. James 'Jimmy' Lomas [Salford] was the first captain of a British Northern Union touring side and Bert Jenkins of Wigan was the leading try scorer with 14 tries, Lomas the top goal kicker with 53. Tours continued at regular four years intervals, except for the two World Wars, virtually to the start of Super League. Among many historic test matches and great wins for Great Britain, two stand out. One on the 1914 tour, the third and final test at Sydney with the tests standing at one each, became known as 'The Rorkes Drift Test' after the heroic stand by a handful of British soldiers who held out against thousands of Zulu warriors. The tourists, down to 10 men for most of the second half and even reduced to nine men for a period, held on for a wonderful 14–6 win. The tourists had been subjected to a fierce playing itinerary and requested a postponement of this test to get a decent team together because of injuries but the Aussies refused and cabled the RFL in Leeds demanding the game should be played. The RFL agreed with their Australian counterparts and cabled the tour manager instructing him to play the match and added the Nelson touch by ending the cable with the words, 'England expects every man to do his duty'. This they did in great style. In future passages in books, whenever a British player was mentioned who had played in this Test match, the initials 'RD' would be printed beside his name. This stood for 'Rorkes Drift', a wonderful honour.

Again in 1958 in Brisbane the team went on to a magnificent victory of 25–18. This was with one man down after 15 minutes and the captain, Alan Prescott, breaking his arm badly after two minutes. Three men were hospitalised after the game. The heroic Prescott played on throughout the full 80 minutes. This game was known as the 'Second Rorkes Drift'. The 'tour trial' games were the main system of tour selection, as well as a great money spinner. Usually one game, and very occasionally two games, might be played on a Wednesday afternoon shortly before the touring side was announced. Teams were selected on club form for these seriously performed and hard fought games and many a player on the fringe of selection has outplayed an opponent considered a 'certainty' and gained selection before him.

To claim to be a Lion, one must have played in a genuine tour which included international Test matches, or on World Cup duty, in some capacity as player, coach, physio or in some managerial position. It was, and still is, a superb accolade to be acclaimed as a Lion. The honour was so sought after and competition for places so fierce that the tour trials were played as a way to analyse last minute form and check fitness to give the maximum chance to any prospective tourist to stake a claim for a place on the trip of a lifetime. When the selected squad was published there was always a surprise choice or two, thanks to the tour trials and sometimes the unusual selection went on to become a household name within the game. The golden rule of tourists, held to this day, is 'What happens on tour, stays on tour'. In other words, no tales are told of what went on away from football in the player's private time. The Lions club, an association of former and current Lions tourists, is thriving today just as strong as the first reunion which took place at Belle Vue, Manchester in November 1945.

The 'genuine' tours of Australia and New Zealand were made in our summer and the trip started immediately at the end of our, then, winter season. The last successful tourists to win the 'ashes' down under were the 1970 team captained by Frank Myler [St Helens], managed by Mr Jack Harding [Leigh] and coached by Johnny Whiteley the former international and Hull FC loose forward. Johnny not only coached the team, he was the assistant manager, conditioner and physiotherapist amongst many other duties. Throughout the full tour their magnificent record was, played 24, won 22, lost 1, drawn 1, losing to Australia in Brisbane in the first Test, 37–15 and drawing against New South Wales in Sydney, 17 all. John Atkinson [Leeds] played in 18 of the games and was the back with most appearances and Jimmy Thompson [Featherstone

Rovers] and Bob Irving [Oldham] topped the games played on tour by forwards with 17 each out of the 24 games played by the team.

There are humorous tales from tours like the one from Ken Gee the strong Wigan prop whose Test prop partner on the 1946 tour was the 17 stone Frank Whitcombe of Bradford Northern. The late Ken used to tell of the Aussie supporter stood near the players' gate at Sydney Cricket Ground when the British team walked out with big Frank and the equally big Ken one behind the other. 'Blimey, look at those two fat Poms and I thought they were starving over in the UK,' shouted the Aussie fan and the crowd screamed with laughter.

Ken agreed afterwards that, weighing in around 34 stones between them, 'The Aussies must have thought we were living like kings and not on ration books as we were'.

Not all tours were happy ones. The 1970 tour was a huge success both on and off the field as was the 1962 tour. The 1958 tour which included the infamous 'Second Rorkes Drift' Test was saved from disaster when a section of the players withdrew their threat to return home because of poor food and the Draconian methods used, early on, by the first ever coach of a touring team the legendary former international and 1936 tour captain, Jim Brough (the then Workington Town team manager). A crisis meeting between players and staff resolved the matter and the heat went out of the row when coach Brough took his Test team away to prepare for the vital third Test with the series hanging at one Test each. This was the first time ever that the tourists were split but it did the trick to give Britain the ashes.

The 1954 Tour was unusual because of a key match of the Tour which was abandoned due to fighting. The game was against the tough New South Wales State side and the Aussies liked to pitch their strong State team against the tourists the week before a Test match. Britain had previously played the New South Wales team the week before the first Test in Sydney and the Aussies beat us 37–12. We won the second Test in Brisbane by 38–21 so the third Test was the decider. The aborted State game was played in Sydney immediately prior to the deciding Test and it was a running battle from the kick off. The referee, Mr Aubrey Oxford, had already dismissed Warrington's dynamic stand off half, Ray Price, for abusive language when, on 56 minutes, he was unable to stop the full scale 25 man battle that started with a one on one fight between Alf Burnell [Hunslet] and Clive Churhill [South Sydney]. Within seconds the Cricket Ground was a battlefield with individual fights and mass brawls going on all over. Mr Oxford blew his whistle and declared the game over and void. The referee officially sent off all the 25 players. A few days later, Australia beat Britain by 20–16 to take the ashes.

On the 1936 tour, captained by Jim Brough [Leeds], the Aussies introduced a tough prop and ex boxer, Ray Stehr. Ray was a handful in a scrap and in the first Test he took on the equally tough Nat Silcock [Widnes] and both walked. Stehr had done a lot of damage in that first Test and, so the legend goes, the managers asked for a volunteer from amongst the British forwards to 'see to' Mr Stehr as early as possible in the second Test. The volunteer was big Jack Arkwright [Warrington] and Jack obliged. Stehr was carted off, never to return that day and Britain won 12–7 in Brisbane. The third Test again played into British hands when big Ray was hell bent on retribution and again Jack Arkwright accommodated him but both were sent off thus allowing Britain to take the ashes with a 12–7 win.

Only three players kicked over 100 goals on all tours. The great Jim Sullivan [Wigan] kicked 110 when captain of the 1932 Tour and in 1954 Lewis Jones kicked 127 goals, a record that looks like staying forever and in 1958 Eric Fraser (Warrington) kicked 110. Mick Sullivan holds the record for most tries on a tour with 38 in 19 games on the 1958 Tour.

The days of close run games in Test match Rugby League between Britain and Australia seem to have disappeared in the mists of time as the green and gold of the Aussie reigns supreme. They are so much quicker and well organised that it seems they may never be caught. The system we are using to develop our youngsters is taking a long time to come into fruition. Each season that goes by seems to increase Australia's grip on international rugby league. Our own traditions are now scorned as old fashioned and out of date. Possibly they are. But without traditions one has nothing to fall back on to find the answers to crucial questions. We have sacrificed our inborn skills and natural aptitude for the game by embracing the alien concept of all-powerful athletes who can perform wonders of lifting and rowing in the gym. By accepting this training discipline at all levels of our game we have almost suffocated the natural born gifts displayed by players like Alex Murphy, Lewis Jones, Gary Schofield, Billy Boston, Dave Valentines, Johnny Whiteley, Vince Karalius, Derek Turner and Ken Gee to attempt to play the Aussies at their own game. Gone are the clever half backs to the almost extinction of the stand off. Our brand of short forward play and the deft pass out of the melee of the tackle to a supporting forward has been exchanged for the Aussie style of, as they term it, taking it in 'first cab off the rank'. We used to beat this head down, bum up style with in-built intelligent play. Where did it go? Time after time we watch 'safety first' play, five drives and a kick. Then, like breath of fresh air, we see a glimpse of brilliance with an old fashioned pass which changes the direction of play and we think that what we used to see regularly is a brilliant new ploy by one of the regiment of same thinking, brain washed coaches. But no, it's a piece of great play by a player who is experiencing a case of *déjà vu* and remembering what he did when a kid. The quicker we revert to playing naturally the better.

14

OLD GROUNDS AND CLUB SPONSORSHIPS

As in most professional team sports many clubs go through some sticky financial periods. Some recover through shrewd housekeeping but, unfortunately, others fall by the wayside and go out of business. This is always a sad occurrence which causes much heartache to directors, committeemen and of course supporters. Our game of rugby league has had its share of clubs who started brightly but, most of the departed clubs became victims of the two dreaded killers of clubs, lack of support through the turnstiles and insufficient commercial activity to bring in the required finance to support the directors (sponsorships). Gaining sponsorships in an unstable financial climate was virtually impossible for the smaller, less successful clubs in rugby league. The bigger clubs always seemed to struggle through but the 'minnows' had a hard time. This was especially seen in the depression years in this country between the wars, when even paying players' fees was at a low ebb. Taking a leaf out of the soccer book, the clubs in rugby league gradually turned to successful local businesses and, depending on their standing in the town or city, landed lucrative contracts which maintained a healthy club. Those were the days when smoking cigarettes and rather excessive drinking took place, so the breweries and multi million pound tobacco companies splashed out excellent sponsorships which not only the clubs but the Rugby

Football League latched onto with relish.

A few clubs were in the fortunate position of having other sports at their grounds as well as rugby league and this meant that the rugby league team was usually looked after financially because of this. Take for instance the Leeds club. They were able to run a superb club with help from the revenue gained from ground board advertising at international and county cricket games, especially the televised five day Test matches. That was big money indeed, plus they had a long and lucrative club sponsorship with a national group brewery. Another great help to the club was the very wealthy Taverners club who had Headingley as its HQ and supported both Yorkshire County Cricket Club and Leeds RLFC.

Clubs not only relied on their major sponsor for funds. Component fund raising efforts went on weekly at the clubs with things such as good cash draws, the 'lucky numbers', Christmas draws and raffles and all sorts of fund raisers. When I was the commercial manager at Leeds, I visited Bolton Wanderers to see how their weekly draw was operated and started the 'Loiners Club', a weekly draw with top cash prizes. An offshoot was the 'Junior Loiners', a club for the youngsters who supported Leeds. In those days we had two or three match sponsors and similarly ball sponsors for each home game, of course since Super League, sponsorship has vastly increased with teams in the big league guaranteed TV time. This makes sponsorship from local and national companies so much easier to gain. At the smaller clubs, it was heartening to receive donations each season from wonderful supporters who were well into retirement but had supported their club since childhood. Every year they would send a cheque for £20 or £10, as they continued to support their lifelong favourites. It was very touching.

Whilst coaching at Halifax in the late 1970s the team was struggling for money when a solicitor's letter arrived saying that a long time supporter had sadly died and had bequeathed a substantial sum of money to the club. This was a superb action by the late gentleman who must have held a true passion for the old ground at Thrum Hall. A comparatively new sponsorship which caused upset at clubs was that of motor car deals. Every player wanted a sponsored car. This idea again came from professional soccer which always had a wider spectator base than rugby league with more TV time and a higher general profile. Car sponsorships, before Super League, were very hard to come by. Thoughts of top soccer players driving around in BMWs, Jaguars and super open topped sports cars, made rugby league stars a little envious and it took quite a time before our players were able to stand toe to toe with their soccer counterparts on the sponsored car scene.

We applied to open a weekly market within the precinct of the old McLaren Field ground as a unique fund raising activity when I was general manager–coach at Bramley RLFC. At first our request was denied as the new market was within the encroachment area of the Leeds Market. A friend of mine who served on the Leeds Council contacted me and advised me to read a particular chapter in the *History of the Village of Bramley*. He said that after reading it we may well want to reapply to open the new market. A trip to Bramley library to read the book made my friend's mysterious suggestion crystal clear. A few hundred years ago the plague hit Leeds so badly that people attending the Leeds Market were literally dropping dead amongst the stalls. The stall holders demanded a new site until the plague had passed and the city fathers asked Rothwell, Hunslet and almost every district to help out. These districts were clear of the plague and thought that the dreaded illness would be brought out to them from the city. They all refused Leeds Market's request. Bramley stepped in and saved the day for Leeds Markets by offering land by Bramley Fall Woods on which to bring the Leeds Market until safer times.

After reading this, we reapplied, reminding the Leeds Market committee of Bramley's help in saving the Leeds Market and we were granted permission. We not only had a Wednesday full market but also a car boot sale on Sunday mornings. The founding of these two fund raisers saved the club before the directors sold the old ground to private housing. The new market coincided with a successful run for the team and the late director of the club, Mr Ernest Humphries once paid me a high compliment when he said, 'You have succeeded in filling two things never before filled at this club, the grandstand and the paying in book at the bank'. Ernest was a grand chap. Our jerseys at Bramley proudly carried the sponsorship name 'Bramley Market' across the chest.

Hull Kingston Rovers were the first club to utilise their big car park at their new ground for a market and car boot sale area and that too helped them financially. At Bramley we had a Big Wheels Show that tore up the playing area but made a few quid for the club. The show consisted of huge vehicles smashing into each other and all sorts of car crashes performed on the playing area. Being the groundsman, amongst other jobs, I was astonished at how little serious damage was done to the playing area. I had to diligently clear away the smashed windscreens and bits of metal from the wrecked cars to ensure visiting clubs made no complaints.

Arranged deals also worked between supporters clubs with hilarious effects and I remember when coaching Leeds RLFC, the Headingley supporters had a 'swap' deal with Featherstone Rovers for their Christmas Raffle (which brought in a good income for most clubs each year). When I called at the supporters club just before Christmas, I noticed the results of the 'Grand 'Fev' Xmas Draw' to which many of the Leeds supporters had subscribed, pinned up on the club's notice board. The first prize was a fish and chip supper at Joe's Fish Shop in Featherstone's main street, the second prize was a pair of motor cycle gauntlets! Would it be reasonable to ask the winner to travel from Leeds to Featherstone for a fish and chip supper? Also not many folk drove motor cycles in the mid 1980s. But it all made for good relations between clubs as well as helping to sell the raffle tickets. These were just a few of the goings on in the world of sponsorships and fund raising as the Rugby Football League clubs came to terms with the comparatively new concept of selling their clubs to the public. These activities all helped the struggle against the giant wave of sponsorships earned in those days by the ever popular soccer 'big hitters'. The appointment of David Howes at RLHQ brought a new dimension for our game as it went into the realms of big money sponsorships and opened the doors for each club to gain these, in many ways, life saving sponsorship packages.

During the long and fateful first 100 winters when our game was born, developed and attained manhood, we have seen two world wars, 1914–18 and 1939–45, the second Boar War 1899–1902, the Korean War 1950–53 and many smaller, yet equally sad conflicts in which rugby league men and women displayed great courage. Some rugby league men gained wonderful awards such as the Victoria Cross and Military Cross for valour and bravery beyond the call of duty. We have seen two Queens, Victoria and Elizabeth II and four Kings, Edward VII, George V, Edward VIII and George VI. We also witnessed a complete alteration to our game with the advent of summer rugby and full time employment for players and staff at clubs. We also saw law and rule changes galore through the 100 winters, each one aimed at improving the game for the paying public. Possibly the hardest factor to accept is that in such a length of time, some clubs would disband and leave the family of our game. Departures have occurred since the initial breakaway at varying intervals. Of the 21 clubs represented at that first historic meeting at the George Hotel, Huddersfield on 29 August 1895, Brighouse Rangers, whose representative, Mr H.H. [Harry] Waller chaired the meeting, Liversedge, Tyldesley, Manningham and Broughton Rangers are no longer operating within the Rugby Football League although Brighouse Rangers still play at a good level of amateur rugby league.

The names of teams who tried out this new form of the handling code make strange reading now as we embrace teams from France, Australia, Papua New Guinea, Tonga, Samoa and many other countries. But local villages and small north country towns flocked to join this new and welcome concept. Today one drives through these villages and towns without giving a thought to their rich rugby football history. At the turn of the nineteenth century they defied the threats of a southern loaded dictatorship to take a step into the future and embrace the democratic freedom of the Northern Union. These names are unknown today yet all clambered on board to join the bright new prospect that would become known as the Northern Game: Melbourne, Fairburn, Ossett, Alverthorpe, Windhill, Kirkstall St Stephens, Hebden Bridge, Normanton, Pontefract, Doncaster Town, Leeds Parish Church, Holbeck who changed codes to become Leeds City then Leeds United and Heckmondwike.

Among the clubs who joined the Yorkshire Senior Competition were two clubs, Bramley and Castleford, who later became staunch clubs in the Rugby Football League. The Lancashire Senior Competition welcomed in Runcorn, a very strong side, Lancaster, Fleetwood, Birkenhead, Dalton, Crompton, Birkenhead Wanderers, Millom, Radcliffe, Altrincham, Leigh Shamrocks, Whitworth, Barton, Walkden, Barrow, Ulverston and St Helens Recreation. The last team mentioned, St Helens Recs, run by the giant glass works, Pilkington's, were admitted into the Rugby Football League proper in 1918–19 and were a strong side in the league for 20 seasons, coming out of the league in 1938–39. In those early years a few Welsh teams entered the Northern Union and in the seasons 1907 to 1909, Merthyr Tydfil, Ebbw Vale, Aberdare, Barry, Mid-Rhondda and Treherbert all joined but none were successful. Coming towards the modern era, Cardiff joined in 1951–52 and went out the same season, then joined again as Cardiff City and played at Ninian Park in 1981–82 and changed to Bridgend in 1984–85 but came out the same season. In 1926–27 Pontypridd came and went in just over one season.

London teams attempted to gain a toehold for the game in the shape of Acton and Willesden and Streatham and Mitcham in the 1935–36 season but Acton and Willesden lasted only one season and Streatham and Mitcham only two. Kent Invicta were formed in 1983–84 and changed to Southend Invicta in 1984–85 but again folded at the end of the first season. The big step forward down south was made when the Fulham club was founded in the 1980–81 season. After lots of ups and downs and name changes, Fulham to London Crusaders to London Broncos and finally to Harlequins RL the club found its way into the 'big league'.

The game of Rugby Football was always strong in Cumberland. That county also had quite a few clubs in the membership of the new Union. Around 1898, clubs such as Seaton, Wath Brow, Whitehaven and Maryport were playing and the county of Cumberland was admitted into the county championship. Much later Workington Town 1945–46, Whitehaven 1948–49 and later still Carlisle 1981–82, entered rugby league.

Two damaging periods caused many teams to withdraw. Firstly the decision in 1902 to create two divisions from the 'bigger' clubs led to the demise of a number of 'junior' clubs who had joined both the Yorkshire and Lancashire Senior Competitions Seconds. These leagues played just beneath the main leagues but still relied on the good fixtures that brought financial stability from within their league. A blow was dealt to the hard working clubs of Chorley, Blackpool Gladiators (the former Blackpool Borough club that had become, in turn, Springfield Borough, Chorley Borough and Trafford Borough) and Nottingham who were cruelly axed from the league in the early 1990s. Prescot followed later after evolving through a series of clubs, Wigan Highfield, London Highfield, Liverpool Stanley, Liverpool City, Huyton and Runcorn Highfield. Mansfield 'Marksmen' lasted a few seasons in the mid 1980s but low gates and poor results caused them to disband.

Several clubs have disbanded and returned. Bradford Northern collapsed twice. Their first collapse was in 1907 when they went out as 'Bradford' and came back as Bradford Northern in 1907. Their second collapse was when they went out during the 1963–64 season and reformed in 1964–65 as, again, Bradford Northern. Hunslet disbanded in 1972–73, reformed in 1973–74 as New Hunslet reverting back to Hunslet later to play at Elland Road then to their current ground at the South Leeds Stadium. Castleford originally performed in the league from 1896 to 1906, then came back after 20 years in 1926 having been reformed as a junior club in 1912. Broughton Rangers, the Salford-based side so successful in the early years transferred to the Belle Vue speedway, fun fair and zoo complex in Manchester in 1933. They consequently changed their name to Belle Vue Rangers in 1946 but disbanded in 1955.

The grounds that have gone remain in the hearts of the thousands of supporters whose club was their major meeting place and part of their very culture. The Parkside ground at Hunslet, like a lot of grounds in Yorkshire, was back to back with the local cricket ground and was a superb complex. It had a line of fir trees at the famous end of the ground known as 'Mother Benson's End'. I remember when I was a youngster there was a cottage on a rise above the ground where Mother Benson lived. The joint grounds which spring to mind are Headingley with its Test cricket oval, Fartown at Huddersfield where Yorkshire played at county cricket level, Halifax at Thrum Hall which had a superb cricket field, Keighley with the big cricket field adjacent, Batley at Mount Pleasant and the beautiful cricket ground side by side with the rugby field. Luckily Keighley and Batley are still with us but the old Parkside ground had a fine, unique, all timber pavilion in which both the rugby and cricket teams changed. The rugby team walked out of the pavilion facing the cricket ground and entered the playing field through the spectator packed terrace by way of a wicket gate. Another great ground that was a throwback to the breakaway years was the old Barley Mow at Bramley. Here too the players entered the playing area through the crowd at the pub end and the pitch was immediately behind the pub building, in the back yard as it were. The public house that served for so long as the headquarters and dressing rooms for the club is still there, on the south side of Town Street. In the next field along was McLaren Field onto which Bramley moved in the mid 1960s. A new grandstand was built and McLaren Field maintained a lot of the charm that had been the Barley Mow. Sadly Bramley's neat ground is now a housing estate and the glorious Parkside is an industrial estate site.

At my last visit, some years ago, the old St Helens Recs ground was still a rugby league ground used by an amateur side. The beloved Fartown still exists—the ground saw so many great entertaining football sides rich in international and local talents. Huddersfield Giants as they are now known play at the magnificent Galpharm Stadium and ground share with Huddersfield Town. A great loss to our game was the selling of one of our finest grounds, Station Road, Swinton. This palatial ground held Test matches against the Australians and New Zealanders, semi-finals and finals galore and had a big, wonderful playing area and an immense ground capacity. Another old favourite was the Athletic Grounds, the home of Rochdale Hornets which also was a huge complex in open ground. The Hornets moved lock, stock and barrel to play at the Rochdale Soccer club's ground, Spotland. Dewsbury played on the sloping Crown Flatt pitch that held the famous 'nine 'ole'. Not only was there a pronounced slope but the bottom corner of the field dropped further to the extent that only half of the corner flag could be seen from ground level. Legend had it that various bones of prop forwards were found in the 'nine 'ole'. This was another ground lost in a housing site but the club moved into the then new Tetley's Stadium in the Shaw Cross area of the town.

Another tragic loss to the game was the selling of Thrum Hall, the stronghold of Halifax RLFC. This old pitch sloped a bit too, down to the pavilion which served as dressing accommodation for the cricket team and the blue and whites. One of the most fearsome grounds to visit was the Boulevard, home of Hull FC. The awesome 'Threp'ney Stand' full of the various dockworkers would greet the teams and woe-betide any visiting player who fouled a Hull man. In the same context, the Boulevard fans were renowned for their support of the team playing the better football and would cheer the opposition to a man if they were outplaying Hull FC. Hull FC's near neighbours, Hull Kingston Rovers, left their home ground of Craven Park for new premises. The old ground, surrounded by a greyhound track, was accepted as a ground on which a side could play open rugby as it was flat and wide. Another fine ground with a slope was the home of a real tough side, Oldham, who played at the Watersheddings, a ground on the slopes of the Pennine moorland. This ground was also replaced by houses. Warrington moved from their long time home at Wilderspool to the brand new Halliwell Jones Stadium whilst Widnes' old traditional ground at Naughton Park was redeveloped to become the excellent Halton Stadium. The grand old York club had a short spell in the financial doldrums after leaving their grand Clarence Street ground and moving well away from the city to the Huntington Stadium in the suburbs. Possibly the most wrenching move was by the famous Wigan club. Their wonderful Central Park is now a Tesco Super Store and the scene of the great achievements of Jim Sullivan, Ces Mountford, Ken Gee, Joe Egan, Brian Nordgren, Eric Ashton and Billy Boston is now a huge car park. This is sad, but I suppose one would say it is progress as the fabulous Wigan now play at the superb JJB Stadium, not too far away from past glories at the great old ground.

Despite new laws and ground regulations relating to Super League, some of the old grounds remain. St Helens are still, at the time of writing, at Knowsley Road, Leeds are at Headingley, Bradford are at Odsal, Wakefield are at Belle Vue, Salford are at The Willows formally Weaste, Castleford are down t'lane at Wheldon Road, Leigh are at Hilton Park, Batley are at Mount Pleasant, Featherstone are at Post Office Road, Barrow are at Craven Park and Keighley are at Lawkholme Lane. The remainder have moved grounds from their original homes to join up with soccer or rugby union clubs or, again, built completely new grounds. Whilst these new ventures are to be applauded, the feeling of entering the old traditional grounds is now just a sadly missed experience. For instance at the old Barley Mow ground, one was so close to the action that one could smell the olive oil and wintergreen emerging from the scrum and hear the sets of forwards speaking to each other as they clashed. You could watch steam rise from 12 strong men who then settled before striving might and main, in a titanic struggle to gain possession of the ball in a competitive scrum. It was wonderful stuff.

Losing the competitive scrimmage saw a massive change to the game as a whole after almost 100 years of this being the method of bringing the ball back into play after a breakdown of handling skills or the ball being put into touch. Losing the amateur tradition after 100 years of holding down a job away from football, yet receiving payment for representing a club on a Saturday afternoon, holiday weekday or over the festive season of Christmas was another traumatic fence to climb for the old traditionalists.

The old game is still missed by the group of senior supporters. These supporters still remember those cold, wet, snowy, wonderful Saturday afternoons in the months from November to March when we ached to watch Wigan, Featherstone, Wakefield, Leeds, Hunslet, Bradford, Warrington, Saints, Swinton, Leigh, Huddersfield, Salford, Castleford and the rest. The anticipation of an exciting match at the weekend warmed us up during the week. Then we would talk about that game until the following Thursday when the topic changed to who we were due to play against at the coming weekend. Our game was the king when sometimes players played three games in three days and cup ties, if drawn, were replayed on the following Wednesday afternoon before huge crowds. Despite the muddy conditions, the 30, 40 or 50 competitive scrums and the regular penalties given for scrimmaging misdemeanours, the massive crowds were entertained. The little men with number 6 on their backs displayed wizardry, another little man wearing number 7 showed constructive guile. Then there was the unselfish running and passing, yes passing, of numbers 3 and 4 and the evasive qualities of pace, strength, swerve, side step, changes of pace and, in a lot of cases, the kicking ability of numbers 2 and 5. Luckily those 'young' enough to have witnessed both eras and understand what we were looking at can compare the two and decide which had more to offer the average supporter. It is hard to compare the two, indeed impossible, without witnessing the two superb games. What we must do is keep the traditions of the old game and marry them to the traditions being made by today's players.

15

POWER OF
THE MEDIA

The part of the game concerned with the media changed more than any other over the first 100 winters. One may say it had to change in the advent of TV coverage but in 1895 the newspapers told of the deeds of the various crowd favourites. Because of the bad blood between north and south over the split, the London and Southern-based newspapers would not even consider giving the fledgling new Northern Union a mention as the Southern broadsheets were members of the establishment. The smaller northern-based newspapers published what the thousands of spectators of this exciting new concept of rugby football wanted to know about the transfers, new signings, weekend teams and any gossip they could get hold of about their heroes. As a youngster in Leeds I had the benefit of two evening newspapers, the *Yorkshire Evening Post* and the *Yorkshire Evening News*. Both publications had covered the game since becoming available to the working classes and the sports reporters usually covered cricket in the summer and soccer and rugby league in alternate weeks. As the game developed in the north, one or two reporters began to specialise in writing about it and in my youth the rugby league man at the *Evening Post* was that well respected journalist, John Bapty. Down to earth Arthur Haddock was the rugby league man for the *Evening News* and he was also held in high esteem by fellow journalists.

In the green sports papers, that was the distinctive colour, on Saturday evenings one could read reports on all the local games of soccer and both codes of rugby football and gain all the classified results of the afternoon's matches. Inside the newspaper were independent pages for each sport. These included all the gossip and latest news from one's own club and it was interesting to see what was happening at other clubs in the area. The reporters who penned these columns of news from the clubs usually wrote under a pseudonym, possibly a throwback to the early days of the game when journalists could have been 'black balled' if they were seen supporting the new game. In the *Evening Post* the writer chose the name, 'Little John', and was of course, John Bapty. The club news covered all the clubs in the county, each one having its own writer.

Our game was very much under subscribed in the marketing stakes then, so much so that the game of rugby league shared a monthly magazine with the most obvious 'bent' sport in the world, professional wrestling. The front half went under the title of *The Rugby League Gazette* and the second half of the magazine was called *The Mat*. The old *Rugby Leaguer* was for many years the only weekly publication devoted to the game. As kids, someone would go to the local 'bug hutch' cinema on the Monday night and on the Pathe news would be a snippet of a game from the Cup Final or Championship Final. This youngster would inform the school that this game was on at the pictures but as Pathe news changed on a Wednesday we broke our necks to get to the cinema, not to watch the film but just to see our game on the big screen. A couple of publications tried to emulate the *Rugby Leaguer* but the *Rugby Leaguer* had cornered the better writers and was well set.

The transfer market generated the biggest news from clubs in those days, they dictated which player was leaving and, more importantly, who was coming. The results mattered but come

Monday they were old news. The news of injuries to players was important but the local newspapers covered that so the most vital stuff a reporter had to offer were the teams for Saturday. Very occasionally news from the Wigan and St Helens camps might hit the nationals but this would only consist of a paragraph or two and cover something important like a cup tie or a derby match. Newspaper coverage in local weekly newspapers was also of vital importance to the avid supporter. Joe Leech was a superb writer for the long lost *Wigan Examiner* and when his distinguished writing career ended, only then did his name figure as the great biographer of rugby league in the Wigan district. As mentioned before, almost every writer on our game was anonymous at the time of writing but Joe Leech was years ahead of his time in the content of his totally understandable and interesting articles.

One of the problems the Southern newspapers had in reporting the northern game in the period before, after and during the two world wars until the 1970s or 1980s was the long winded system of reporting provincial news that the newspaper world had adhered to since the stone age. Important reports of games were telephoned to a copy typist in a local news office say in Manchester, then that copy would go to every man and his dog to be checked and edited to fit the demands of the various editions of the newspaper. By the time it hit London it was either old news or the editors of the uneducated South couldn't tell rugby league news from the price of cod at Hull docks. Thanks to Eddy Shah the newspaper industry finally came into the twentieth century as late as the 1980s after he won the battle to introduce modern technology into the whole of the newspaper industry.

Rugby league specialists like Roger Halstead of the *Oldham Evening Chronicle*, Dick Tingle of the *Hull Daily Mail*, the great golfer and Wigan man, John Robinson of the *Sunday People*, Brian Batty of the *Daily Mail* and the experienced Jack McNamara of the

Manchester Evening News are thin on the ground these days. This is because the specialist rugby league writers were the first to feel the axe of progress as the nation wanted to know what the Manchester United team had for breakfast rather than what was happening in the fully professional game of rugby league. It is well known that pre-1995 a journalist could get a quote from a player only minutes before a game. Now in the ultra professional press conference after the games most times the coach will send his assistant to face the barrage of questions who almost always answers with the same clichéd remarks. Hardly anything is true according to the coaches and it is as if nothing should be given away that might appear in tomorrow's newspapers.

TV's input to the 'opening up' of our game has been huge. Initially the BBC captured the Challenge Cup games and particularly the Wembley finals. The Beeb also sponsored a very popular competition, the BBC Floodlit Trophy for a few years. Later the Sky Corporation gained control of the bigger league games to offer the rugby league supporter hours of entertainment in the comfort of their own home. There were various offshoots of programmes dealing with both the local and international face of the game. The man still remembered by the older end of the supporters as the voice and face of the game was the late, great Eddie Waring. A journalist turned TV personality, Eddie was the first reporter to tour with the 1946 Lions tour of Australia and New Zealand and his brand of home spun northern humour was just right for his time of popularity. Ray French was the next regular commentator who brought with him an ex–player's view as his cultured, though still Lancashire, dialect was soon accepted. Ray's job was a hard one as Eddie had commentated for so long that he had become a legend. At the time it was considered that nobody would be able to 'follow that' but Ray did with aplomb.

ITV found it difficult to find a niche because of first the BBC watertight contracts and then the influx of Sky TV. Keith Macklin, another well respected and experienced journalist, was an excellent 'caller' of games both on radio and TV. Local radio stations made a big impact by broadcasting live games each weekend and some first class reporters honed their skills at grounds throughout the north at the microphones of Radio Leeds, Radio Pennine, Radio Aire, GMR and Radio Cumbria. Other smaller stations also covered weekly rugby league.

I feel the game started to lose its characters at the advent of Super League. Until then reporters could get earthy, down to the bone and obtain honest reaction from most coaches. They captured real heart on the sleeve stuff with no punches pulled. Now responses are inclined to be robotic and predictable. The influx of Australian coaches brought an increase in eloquence when speaking to reporters, mainly because that skill had been honed in the strong media pull the game has had in Australia since its inception. Most Australian players were better schooled in talking to the media than British players and whilst our homebred men mumbled and shuffled around, obviously not used to the mike or the camera, the overseas players, in some cases, were better than the reporter. We have improved over the years but the confident Aussies and Kiwis are still there among us.

The power of the press is far greater now than it was sat the end of the first 100 winters. Media coverage today is stronger than ever and it now includes the internet and email, where individual clubs fire out messages on club lines over computers. This gives more opportunities for the spectator to keep up with events at their own club and indeed all around the leagues. Because of this, the players today are not as easy to meet and talk to as in the earlier period. Now, when the average supporter is at work or the younger ones at school, the players are training. Adults and youngsters can no longer go to a ground and watch their heroes train in the evenings after work or school as they were able to do before full time football employment. Back then a bond of almost knowing the players personally grew with the supporters and this cemented the close family-type spectator involvement. This has been lost forever. The complete media component of the game has grown out of all proportion, huge teams of non specialists now record match reports using overseas jargon and have produced, over the past few years, a language which would have left the former players and coaches, of only 10 years ago, wondering what on earth they were talking about. But that, so they say, is progress.

16

FROM TIN BATHS
TO SHOWERS

The old adage that no one was ever born a professional at any sport is true. The need for an amateur section to work in unison with the professionals is essential in all sports. Schools play a big part of a child deciding which sport they will follow into adulthood. A teacher interested enough to give advice to pupils about which sport to enter is worth their weight in gold. If the school does not follow a sport in which a pupil wants to participate then a good teacher will guide that pupil to the nearest club practising that particular sport. Most schools offer some sort of individual or team sport for the pupils to take an interest in. Grammar and public schools were normally rugby union and cricket orientated. Intellectual students went on to university where they continued their chosen sport. State schools usually focused on soccer, rugby league and cricket. Whether a school played soccer or rugby league depended on the interest of the teacher in charge of sport or the geographical area a school was in.

As a kid in Leeds if a school was situated in the Elland Road district, namely Holbeck, Wortley and Beeston, then you played soccer. If your school was in the Kirkstall, Burley or Headingley district then you played rugby league. There were few options in the south Leeds district of Hunslet as even the girls had to play rugby league, hence the superb district of Hunslet produced more great rugby league players in its domain than some of the complete big cities in Yorkshire. Young school children gained their fill of rugby league by playing for their school and, if lucky, for their city team. Hunslet had a city team whilst being a suburb of Leeds city.

Just after the Second World War, there was little or no junior rugby league for a youngster to play after the (then) school leaving age of 14, later 15. The amateur leagues worked out a club and league system that started in Leeds and its districts in 1951. Under 17 leagues catered for school leavers at 15 years old to 16-and-a-half years old. Then one moved to the under 18-and-a-half league, then into the open age league. It seemed to be a natural progression. A player was allowed to sign as a professional player, with parental permission, at 17 years old. In 1951 at most junior clubs the conditions for training, travelling and playing were archaic. The clubs lucky enough to be associated with professional clubs had decent training facilities but apart from a few games allowed on the club's main pitch as curtain raisers all other games were played on park pitches.

My club, Headingley Juniors, had the use of a pitch close to the Headingley ground on Becket Park but our reserve ground was on the other side of Leeds at Roundhey on what was known as Soldiers Field. We made this journey on the old tram car but there were no changing facilities at all and our team's reserve had to guard our clothes on the day. Travelling back to Headingley on the tram was uncomfortable, especially on a muddy afternoon, as one sat with one's trousers covering filthy legs as there were no washing facilities. The team had to mind its P's and Q's so it wouldn't be thrown off the tram due to our filthy condition.

I was lucky enough to be signed as a professional at 17 years old whilst some of our very good side, not fancying the brutal open age league at 18 years old, opted for the rugby union game. Other players finished completely with the game. The conditions in the open age divisions were little better than conditions in the junior divisions in some cases. Some firms ran teams and in fairness the dressing and bathing facilities were acceptable—at others they were excellent. Chances of advancement in the amateur game in those days were limited. County selection for one's home county was a fine achievement and the ultimate honour was selection for the England Amateur Rugby League team which in those days only played in France. Public houses were still the most popular home headquarters for teams in amateur rugby league.

Although the local challenge cups in the various leagues were held in high esteem, the two biggest annual competitions were the County Cups. If teams reached the first round proper of the Rugby League Challenge Cup, the end product was playing at Wembley. This was some dream indeed as only a handful of amateur sides have ever gone into the hat for the old round two. In those far off days, the Rugby League Challenge Cup qualifying rounds started long before the first round proper in February. Two teams from the hundreds of amateur sides entering, one each from the Yorkshire and Lancashire competitions, went through to take on the professionals. The Cumberland county sides played in the Lancashire section. Getting through to the first round proper meant a huge cash windfall for the amateurs and usually paid for a couple of new playing strips, took care of two or three years of players' insurance and added a few quid in the bank. Most amateur clubs, to this day, hold the team that represented their club in the first round proper all those years ago in great respect. Usually there are a few old photographs hung on the clubhouse wall of the successful team.

Things happened over the years and moving into the early 1970s the amateur game was in disarray. Clubs disbanded regularly as they had little help from the professional game. At that time the senior clubs had to look to themselves regarding finances as their section of the game was going through a sticky patch. A group of staunch rugby league men met to see if they could run the amateur game as a separate entity away from the professional body in Chapeltown Road, the then HQ of the game. Meetings between the amateur spokesmen and the professional management committee were held and at first no agreeable decision could be reached as there was a feeling of mistrust. But, as in 1895, the hundreds of amateur teams, for the first time in around 80 years, broke away and stood on their own two feet. They organised their own game and did a great job. With massive assistance from the newly formed Sports Council, advice and financial grants, the British Amateur Rugby League Association came into being and with it came hundreds more junior teams at ages never before envisaged. There was even space for girls to play if they wanted!

The international fixtures and tours spread from not only playing France but New Zealand, Australia, New Guinea, the South Pacific, South Africa, Russia and many more countries. Ladies teams emerged and also played abroad at international level and the Army, Navy and Air Force now play. Before BARLA, only rugby union was allowed. Rugby league development officers were appointed in city leisure services and thousands of children began playing the game. BARLA also fought tooth and nail to gain a free gangway for players between league and union, never before allowed by Twickenham.

Amateur clubs now cater for all ages of rugby league football and most clubhouses and dressing accommodation are state of the art. Two of the most impressive clubhouses in the area in which I live are at the Castleford Lock Lane Sports Centre and at the imposing complex that is now the Stanningley Amateur Rugby League Club. Both are a credit to the hard work and total commitment of the clubs' committees. I had the pleasure and privilege of coaching both these clubs at various times in my coaching career. My first coaching job was at Stanningley and our changing accommodation in those days was very different from the new ground and its superb facilities. Then the changing accommodation was in the cellar of the Wagon and Horses pub. When coaching at Lock Lane our dressing rooms and club HQ were in another old pub which had been purchased by the club committee and renamed 'The Early Bath'. The beauty of these new facilities is that lots of different sports teams use them. In a comparatively short 30 years, the amateur game has taken giant strides and is improving rapidly year by year. The improvement has been a wonderful achievement by an ultra dedicated and clever group of enthusiasts. Today's facilities are a far cry from the tin bath full of icy water occasionally used by players to clean up after a game on a muddy winter's afternoon in those dark, archaic days.

17

LOST SKILLS

I have already mentioned individual sections of lost skills in rugby league. For those people who remember the old skills of the game and for those readers who never saw the old game, I attempt to jog the memory of the former and explain to the latter how things were before 1996. The first skill taught in the Rugby League Coaching Scheme's curriculum was always passing and handling. The basics were similar to most ball games—keep your eyes on the ball. When in possession of the ball use a relaxed grip with both hands, keep your eye on the target area, which is below the chest and above the waist band of the shorts. For a smooth release of the ball, pass across one's tummy with elbows slightly bent and deliver into the target area, not too hard but with the correct weight of pass to make catching the ball easy for the person you are passing to. Keep your eye on the ball when receiving the pass and catch the ball with both hands, caressing the ball into the safety of the hands, arms and chest forming a cradle. This is how we used to teach children but the basics were the same for adult professional players. There were of course various offshoots of passing and handling.

The most common way of changing the direction of a team's attack was the drop off pass where the ball handler would run across the catcher and pass the ball, using the basics of eye on the target area, back to the catcher who would run into the gap that the passer had just left after taking the pass. This is a pass used today but in the old game it was used on more occasions. The centre-wingman combination used a similar pass called the 'scissors move'. The centre would run in a straight line then suddenly veer across towards the near touchline. His wingman timed his inside run to accept the centre's pass and often ran into a gap created by the centre drawing his opposite defender across with him leaving the gap for the wingman to accelerate into. The move was sometimes highlighted when the centre gave a 'back flip' pass out of one hand, his body hiding the pass from the defender. This was a real crowd pleaser. The ideal 'scissors pass' was exactly as described except for the actual pass. The centre would not 'back flip' the pass but would turn his head to find the target area with his eyes before passing to that target area. The 'face pass' was an excellent attacking ploy when passing the ball across one's line of attack and instead of passing to the player next in line, one passed it across the front of him and hit the player next in the line. Usually this player had selected his line of angled run and would race into a gap in the defence.

The 'miss pass' was worked in a totally different way as the passer allowed the next receiver to run past him and hit the next man in the line who would be deeper than the missed man. This pass is still used regularly today. The 'around the tackler pass' is a real defence buster. This pass is performed usually in mid field and the ball carrier deliberately attracts the tackler to him. On contact the ball carrier pulls the tackler to him and simultaneously reaches with the ball in one hand behind the tackler and delivers a pass to a team member in support. This is a difficult pass to perform and only the experienced ball handler and a player who can hold and control the ball in one hand would attempt it but it can be a devastating pass. Many old fashioned forwards were masters of this pass such as Chris Brereton [Leeds] and Ken Gee [Wigan]. Later Kevin Ward [Castleford and Saints] and Bill Ashurst [Wigan and Wakefield] were expert in its use and today Andy Lynch [Bradford Bulls] uses it to good effect. For years rugby union players used the 'spin pass' but its effective use was only recently used in rugby league. It is an accurate pass when long passes are required and its spin is imparted by a flick of the wrists across the line of pass at the split second of release. The 'long pass' is self explanatory in that it cuts out several players and is usually aimed at a team mate in a wide position such as a centre, wingman or a wide running forward.

This skill of support play is married to passing and handling. A player who can 'read' a break and be on hand to accept the final pass to score is worth his weight in gold. These support players are blessed with a gift called awareness. Game awareness cannot be coached. A player either has it or doesn't. There have been plenty of players and there still are one or two players with this in-built skill. Alan Hardisty had it, Danny McGuire has it and it is simply to be in the right place at the right time. The combination of watching a great break or move and then seeing a support player ghosting into a position to take the pass and shoot to the line is one of the many thrills of our game.

Defensive play used to be a skill one could or couldn't do. As a young player in my day, the terms 'Tackle around the legs' and, as the coach and older players would say, 'They can't run without their legs' were about the only words of advice given about defence. No one practised defensive drills or individual tackles. Even when becoming a professional player, defence was never an ultra important factor of coaching. There were old sayings that had hung over since the breakaway, for instance the 'mad dog and paling fence' system. One imagined that your defence was a paling fence and that the opposition ball carrier was a mad dog. If one paling was out of place then the mad dog would get through and bite you. This was simple compared to today's complicated systems, but effective in its simplicity. As the penny dropped on the importance of good defence, we used the 'umbrella' defence in which the two centres, one at either side of the field, would sprint up and slightly inwards taking every team mate with them and forming an inverted umbrella shape into which the opposing attack would be drawn.

There was the 'stacked defence' in which both wingmen pushed infield to make an impassable barrier around the attacking play the ball. This allowed the defensive side to dictate in which area the game would be played. The 'sliding defence' was a ploy that if an opponent passed the ball in front of you, then you simply turned in the direction of the pass, slid across field and defended any move that came back in your direction. Its purpose was to allow the opposition to pass the ball across the field but make little progress through your defensive line. In theory the team carrying the ball would not go forward past your sliding defence. The Australians were particularly adept at 'stacked' and 'sliding' defences. The ideal tackle would be a two man tackle with one going low around the legs to stop the runner's progress and the second going in around the ball to stop any slipped passes. The weak area in British defences was always around the play the ball ruck. We took a long time to come to grips with the 'double marker' system at the play the ball. For years we operated a single marker system with just one marker covering the play the ball. The 1982 Australian tourists cleaned us out around this area by simply having their dummy half run from the base and casually turn the ball back inside when challenged by our one marker. This allowed the support player to break clean through. This was so simple, but we had considered our system unassailable.

Getting forwards to work hard to form a double marker, after years of being able to take it easy and hide away behind the *play the ball*, was almost impossible at first, but now it is second nature. All kinds of systems were tried at double marker, one marker going left the other going right, neither working in the tackle, just covering the gaps at the side of the play the ball and various plays before the current system of hard work and talking to each other came into fruition. We also used a ploy for a few years called a 'bobby'. This was when a player acted as a middle line of defence, behind the front line but in front of the full back. A great example of this was the excellent hooker for Dewsbury and Great Britain, Mick 'Stevo' Stephenson who built his reputation as a brilliant cover tackler on this bobby position. If a wingman or centre broke the front line then Stevo raced across to bring the runner down with a classical tackle but in the bobby position he was 10 yards nearer to the runner than anyone else! To mention a 'cover tackle' may help the senior reader remember second row forwards and loose forwards as cover tacklers. A good back rower, if put out of the game by a pass leaving him, would sprint across the back of his advancing defence and 'corner flag', as we called it and knock anything down that poked through that front line. That was covering. It fell to the back row as they were usually the fastest of the forwards. Bob Haigh of Wakefield Trinity, Geoff Gunney of Hunslet and Brian Briggs of Saints, Wakefield Trinity and Huddersfield were fantastic cover tacklers. The cover tackle is now virtually extinct as defences became almost watertight.

The Australians brought in the 'gang tackle', a brutal three or four man tackle. The first man into the tackle trapped the legs of the ball carrier without knocking him down. The second man in locked the ball in an embrace-like tackle around the ball carrier's body and turned the ball carrier slightly into the path of the third and/or fourth who drove into the ribs or back of the ball carrier with their shoulders. This resulted in quite a few broken ribs and, in some cases, dislocated vertebrae.

In the days of the Northern Union the head high tackle was prevalent with most forwards who had played for a while. The forwards carried the 'badges of honour' such as broken noses and cauliflower ears. Forwards would batter each other in the tackle, as they had done way back in the history of the game. This battering was known as 'softening up' the opposition. The running player with the ball had little to offer in the way of defence against a high head tackle but with time came experience and the forward runners learned how to pick up their knees as they accelerated into a tackle. They also learned how to use their elbow, a tough means of defence as more often than not the tackler, who intended to do the runner harm, ended up with a broken nose, jaw or cheek bone fracture. With perfect timing the ball carrier would lift his arm, bent and beat the thug tackler to the punch as the elbow thudded into his face. A few players mastered of this type of 'self preservation'. The tackler could cause some damage with the elbow. One particular tackle in an Australian State of Origin game saw New South Welshman Les Boyd break the jaw of opposite prop Queenslander Darryl Brohmann.

Old heads, the most experienced players, had lots of ancient methods of making life difficult for the opposition. One was, on a muddy day, to grab a handful of the foul smelling, wet earth and rub it into the face of the tackled player, usually in the melee of a three or four man tangle. Grabbing and twisting the private parts of an opponent was an old method of inflicting pain on the attacking player and eye gouging occurred occasionally, not simultaneously, I might add. The 'old faithful' though was the 'stiff arm' or 'half arm' tackle. As an attacker went in for the tackle, a defender aimed this high tackle and swung his forearm at the throat, mouth, nose or eye of an attacker as he went in for the tackle. It usually caused great consternation amongst the attacking team and its supporters, not to mention the ball carrier.

One of the most awesome tackles was the old 'Cumberland tackle' sometimes called the 'Cumberland throw'. Strangely this was a weapon of the smaller player, picked out by the bigger ball carrier as a target. The tackler moved in slightly to the free hand side of the runner, with the ball carried in the other arm. Then, as the runner introduced his hand off, the tackler grabbed the arm with both hands, threw his inside leg across the front of the runner and simply let the runner's own momentum take him to ground, face first. There was no protection for the face as one arm was in possession of the tackler and the other was carrying the ball! The runner was suddenly in a situation where the ground was coming at him at a fast rate of knots and he could do nothing about it. His face hit the ground and although there would no doubt be heavy conditions underfoot, the tackle, deemed legal, was a frightening experience indeed.

Another unusual feeling was that of being lifted upwards and backwards and having no control of your movement whatsoever by that most dreaded tackle, the 'blockbuster'. A head on tackler, would stoop below balance level, stop their target dead in their tracks and thrust them upwards and backwards with feet off the ground. The victim knew that the next impact would be their back hitting the ground with the weight of the tackler following a split second later, rather like waiting for the dentist to start drilling! The outcome of this tackle could be a bruised spine, slipped disc, broken rib or if the back of the head hit the ground first, concussion.

To try to avoid these bone shaking tackles a player had to evolve some evasive techniques, to use brain instead of brawn. The back line in particular had to acquire the skills to beat a one on one confrontation. Most had a variation of their own on the old methods of evasive tactics, the side step, swerve, dummy pass, change of pace, chip kick over the defence and re-gather, or the evasive tactic for which there is no known answer, sheer unstoppable pace. The forwards' perspective of evasion was totally different to that of the backs. Usually operating in the 'traffic' of their opponents' forwards their thinking had to be slightly different. On attack, the 'hit and spin' tactic worked well. A forward would run full speed at an opponent then hit the tackler with his shoulder at the same time spinning away from the tackle in one loop. The little step off either foot into the gap between two tacklers was another ploy, running as if to move across the tackler then propping off either foot to slice into the gap, freeing arms and hands to hit the area behind the defence and offer a pass to supporting team mates. Short support work running off a ball handler was another ploy and the work of the dummy half was an important piece of the forwards' attacking jigsaw as his swift running from the dummy half position was vital.

A major change that came with Super League was the virtual disappearance of set moves from either the play the ball or the tap penalty. After kicking a penalty kick into touch the tap kick to bring the back ball into play was taken 10 yards infield from the point the ball crossed the touchline from the kick. From this play, if say, anywhere around 30 yards from the opponent's try line, a set move would be put on. Set moves were designed to do various jobs. They either contained the opponents' forwards in one area whilst other members of the team attacked a weaker point in the defensive line, or forced opponents to 'stack in' their defence, then with wide passing, hit them on the far outside. Usually each set move from the tap involved forwards. The run around was used extensively—this was when a player passed to his team mate who took one step forward, the original passer sprinted around the receiver who returned the ball to him, from this play usually another faster forward would come straight and hard onto a short pass from the original passer, into a gap between two defenders. A variation was for the original passer to run square from the run around move and by passing two of his team mates and running across two defenders hit the third man out with a change of direction 'drop off' pass, sending the runner into the gap he had just run across. Almost every move was a variation of the run around or the drop off pass, but any coach worth his salt had many moves for his players to use and practised them regularly.

One special move that was used only when certain occasions

arose, involved a pinpoint kick and took a great deal of courage by the kicker as it involved a high kick to the opponent's posts directly from the tap kick. As coach at Wigan many years ago my side practised this move and code named it 'Shock'. We used it only once in the season and it worked perfectly to beat Leeds in the league at Central Park. Behind by two points and in injury time in the second half, we were awarded a penalty kick which was placed into touch on the Leeds '25' line. My half back took the tap kick and immediately punted high to the Leeds posts. Amid the panic that the kick caused, the Leeds full back dropped the ball and it rolled slowly into the Leeds in-goal area where one of my centres simply dived on the ball to score the winning try. This was the beauty of doing the unusual. So near their line Leeds expected the normal attack from around the tap kick but because of our practice and the code word, 'Shock', my team stacked in on the far side of the field to saturate the area around the posts and the ball duly arrived in that area only thinly defended by Leeds. The French used a variation of the instant kick from the tap when the tap kicker simply turned his back on the opposition defence and put in a cheeky (but well practised) over his shoulder 'backwards' punt. This was a wonderful innovation, rarely seen, but one that the crowd loved and it was another instance of doing the unusual from the tap. With the French forwards charging through and the kick delivered to be inch perfect, it resulted in a try almost every time. But the penalty tap kick occurred only a few times in the whole game in the perfect attacking position.

The place to organise one's set moves was from the scrum and the play the ball. This was the domain of the crafty hookers and scrum halves or the skilful ball playing forward. The set scrum moves usually involved the two half backs and the loose forward and the book was full of ultra intelligent work from the 'eternal triangle' of the numbers 6, 7 and 13. One match winning move between the scrum half and loose forward centred on an accurate reverse or back pass from the half back who ran away from a close in scrum and back flipped a pass to the trailing loose forward. A perfect instance of this move was Great Britain versus Australia at Leeds in 1959 when scrum half Jeff Stevenson's perfect back pass sent in loose forward Johnny Whiteley for the winning try in the final minutes of the game. There were literally hundreds of moves from the play the ball, especially near the opponents' goal line. There were the variations of the criss-cross runners, the sly little back pass from the dummy half to his team mate as he ran across him, the dummy then ducked under the tacklers to score and many more. Sometimes certain moves became the trade mark of a certain hooker or scrum half. The part of the ball playing forward was crucial in and around the play the ball with short passes, delayed passes and every kind of skill in handling which ended mostly with the ball player taking a heavy tackle. The tackler was left frustrated as the ball player released to his mate who was tearing through. During the time of our dominance of the international scene, our game was built on ball handling forwards, crafty scrum halves and constructive stand off halves. The Australians and New Zealanders were in awe of the Great Britain skill in the vital ball playing role. This was until the arrival of the great Arthur Beetson who was a revelation in the Sydney week to week league football with his 'English' style ball handling.

The modern game relies heavily on a skill described as 'the kicking game' but the same kicking skills used in the modern game were in use from day one in the Northern Union. The types of kicking skill were many and varied in that first 100 years. Several remain to this day but, alas, several were discarded in the march of progress. The most skilful facets of the kicking game no longer used were the kicking duals between the opposing full backs. This was started by one full back kicking long to his opposite full back and in a planned move the kicking full back's forwards would have charged up field to 'ring' the catching full back. The forwards had to be at least 10 yards away from the catcher to remain onside and were hoping that he would make a mistake in his fielding of the ball from each kick. As the catching full back had been in splendid isolation he was on his own surrounded by six tough men, all telling him what they would do to him should he 'fluff' his catch. On catching the ball and having nowhere to run, the full back would send in a return kick to the original full back who would now be surrounded by the opposition forwards. The long kickers, as most of the old full backs were, would attempt to move their opposite full back around the field whilst the catcher, on both sides, was still under extreme pressure from the opposite six forwards. The experienced full back would deliberately kick 10 yards shorter, then another 10 yards shorter on his second kick. Just as his opponent thought he was weakening, the experienced man fired in a siege gun spiral kick way over the head of his opponent which would have the other full back scurrying back, hounded by the hungry pack of forwards. One of the finest exponents of this ploy was the fabulous Wigan full back, Jim Sullivan. Soon one or other of the full backs would make a mistake and as the forwards of both teams had had a rest period, they would swoop, regain possession and set up an attack, usually near their opponents' line. Many times a try ensued directly from the dropped ball.

The cross kick is another lost skill. This kick was normally from a wingman, put clear along the touchline. When approached by the opposing cover tackler or the full back the wingman would, without losing speed, punt the ball into the path of his supporting forwards who would be charging up centre field in a line covering a 20 yard area. There would then be a pick up, a short sprint and a try recorded. As a young supporter of the Leeds club I witnessed wingman Ernie Whitehead of Leeds perform this lost skill on many occasions and he was a master of the art. Somehow today we never seem to see a wingman going clear and for him to kick would be sacrilege. The grubber kick is still an attacking weapon, used near the opposing try line these days, but it was used more in the old days by the scrum half. He would collect the ball from a scrum heel, dash around the back of his scrum and grubber ahead, some 15 or 20 yards into touch, saving his pack some hard work.

The forwards' workload was in four major areas, driving the ball out of one's own '25', defence, support play and scrummaging. The skills of the latter are now dead and buried. In the old days an open side prop was the pivot of the scrum. His job in the tight was not just strength but also nimbleness of foot. More often than not he won the ball as he wedged in towards the opposing hooker with his head. He held up the opposing prop, at the same time hooked the ball and supported his own hooker whilst stood on one foot! His body position in the scrum was with his backside away from the rest of the scrum as he, as stated, wedged in on the opposing hooker attempting to lift his head up and out of the scrum. If the open side prop was the pivot, then the blind side prop was the hinge. His job was to get as low as possible and offer his inside leg as a seat for the hooker to sit on and pull, not push, this helped thrust weight towards the open side and create the advantage for his own hooker so that his legs and face were almost at the mouth of the tunnel of the scrum. At some strategic moment, one of the second row forwards might take it upon himself to assist his own hooker by smacking the opposite hooker in the mush with a crafty punch. This was called 'putting one through' and this, too, had a blueprint of how it should be done. The prop, either open or blind side, would be asked to 'open up' and he would oblige by creating a gap between him and the hooker through which the second row forward would throw his Sunday punch. But it was the clash of heads when connecting for the scrum that did the most damage.

The 'Glasgow Kiss' had nothing to compare with the head butting specialists who roamed the front rows then. Most of the mayhem was caused early on in scrimmaging. The concerted pushing and wheeling in the scrum called for immense strength and a substantial amount of a six man skill, all acting in unison with the steam rising from the packs like mum's Monday washing tub. The grappling, heaving mass of 12 huge men belied the intricate pinpoint skills that occurred in the seemingly pointless melee. The hooker was not there to have it easy. He was the contortionist extraordinaire. Bent into incredible shapes, with face inches from the ground, he would strive, might and main, to win the ball. Fast strikers for the ball were like the King Cobra and were incredibly quick and accurate. Devious plans were made between the open side prop and the hooker. The hooker would block his opponent's strike with both his legs and his prop would heel the ball out. Another favourite ploy was to stand up in the scrum and adjust one's shoulder pads then the referee would make the opposition front row stand to allow the hooker back into the scrum and with the elbow still bent from adjusting the pads, he would swing the elbow across hitting the other hooker on its way around the prop's neck.

The spectator's two most hated aspects of the old competitive scrum were 'own feet' where the feeding scrum half put the ball behind his hooker's feet and 'feet across' where the hooker struck early for the ball and both his feet would appear at the tunnel mouth before the ball was put in. No longer do the heartfelt cries of, 'Ger 'em onside ref' ring out from the terraces when a team are in possession or, 'Ger 'is feet back ref' or, ' Own feet ref' when scrimmaging. Competitive scrums were hard places to be in and spectators always gave advice to both players and referees. If a hooker was being beaten for possession some wag would surely shout out, 'Throw a bag of peas in, he's forced to get one of those!' This was cruel, but to the point, as possession was crucial to any team winning any game. Competitive scrums could go either way. Unlike today, a surprise heel near your opponent's try line was unpredictable and this element alone, the game's unpredictability, made for a very different kind of excitement compared to that of today.

The second row forwards each had a different job. The open side second rower's job from a scrum lost was to 'corner flag', that was to cover across the back of his three quarters' defensive line and knock down anything that broke through. The blind side second row man at a scrum lost would quickly check the blind side to make sure no 'traffic' was coming down that dangerous passage and, if not, he would 'corner flag' behind his partner. On attack it was usual to have at least one second rower who was a fast, strong runner. If you had two of these you were blessed. The loose forward could, at one time, stand out of the pack and cover the blind side, especially at a scrum near his own line. Then a change to the laws of scrimmaging forced him to be in the scrum at all times. Whatever the law, his first job was to check the blind side and nail the half back if he ran from the base of the pack. He was usually a good footballer with good hands and a safe defender. On attack he was said to be the link between backs and forwards. In the old days the constitution of a good pack was three tough front rowers who would do the hard donkey work and tackle in the mid-field, the second row partnership would have an out and out runner and a joint runner-tackler and the loose forward, a ball handler who had to tackle.

Players today, so the coaches say, have to be interchangeable but in the old days a full back could get by in the centre and vice versa. Similarly a wingman could manage a game in the centre and the half backs were interchangeable, such as Alex Murphy. The props were also interchangeable at a pinch and a good second rower could manage at number 13 and vice versa. The only position needing an absolute specialist was at hooker. Today this is one of the least specialised positions, for his skills at winning the set scrum are now obsolete, yet most clubs still use the hooker as dummy half at the play the ball and this is a specialised position. It is of the utmost importance to send the attack in the correct direction and the pass from dummy half dictates where the attack is aimed. Running from dummy half is also vital and an eye for an opening is a crucial asset. The great hooker, Tommy Harris of Hull FC was a brilliant exponent of dummy half play, as was Kevin Ashcroft of Leigh and Warrington as well as many more.

In our first 100 years, we had wonderful star quality names who graced the game and became legends. There were players from all over the world as well as local lads, we had players who showed true heroism in two World Wars, Jack Harrison of Hull FC won both the Victoria Cross and the Military Cross for bravery in the First World War. The Principality of Wales contributed superbly in supplying brilliant players, as did Scotland and Ireland. Names that spring to mind from the early years are Harold Wagstaff, Albert Rosenfeld, William 'Billy' Batten, Jim Sullivan, Jimmy Lomas, Ben Gronow, Frank Gallagher, Danny Hurcombe, Jonathan 'Jonty' Parkin, Jim Brough, Gus Risman, Ike Owens, Ernest Ward, Tom Van Vollenhoven, Vince Karalius, Alex Murphy, Brian Bevan, Lionel Cooper, Pat Devery, Johnny Hunter, Arthur Clues, Billy Boston, Neil Fox, Roger Millward, Ellery Hanley, Kevin Ward, Mal Reilly, Trevor Foster, Dick Huddart, Ken Traill, Dave Valentine, Lewis Jones, Eric Ashton, Alan Prescott, Brian McTigue, Johnny Whiteley, Tommy Harris, Derek Turner, Mick Sullivan, Frank Myler, Brian Edgar, Mick Shoebottom, Alan Hardisty, John Atkinson, Alan Smith, Tony Fisher, Kevin Ashcroft, Terry Clawson, Gary Schofield, Des Drummond and Shaun Edwards to mention but a few of the great players who, over 100 hundred years, made our game great.

This trip back to past traditions and the changing face of rugby league over the last 100 years has, I hope, preserved and rekindled some great memories of the old game and old times. The heritage of the old rugby league game needs to be remembered as the new Super League game develops in order to avoid past mistakes being repeated. I hope that by recording my memories of these old times it will help the younger reader comprehend the history and heroics of past rugby league players and how they have all contributed in their own way to today's game. I also hope my memories have reminded older readers of the fantastic times we used to have. Let's hope the next 100 years of rugby league can provide as many great memories and traditions as the first 100 years of rugby league did!